The Enlightened Despots

Frederick the Great and Prussia

Napoleon and Europe

Empires
Their Rise and Fall

The Enlightened Despots

Frederick the Great and Prussia

Napoleon and Europe

Ron W. Walden

Frederick the Great and Prussia

Joyce Milton

Napoleon and Europe

Preface by Daniel Stone
Professor of History
University of Winnipeg

Boston Publishing Company, Inc.
Boston, Massachusetts

Empires: Their Rise and Fall is published in the United States by Boston Publishing Company, Inc., and distributed by Field Publications.

Authors: Ron W. Walden, Joyce Milton
Picture Researcher, Janet Adams
Historical Consultant, Professor James Miller
Project Consultant, Valerie Hopkins
Design Implementation, Designworks

Boston Publishing Company, Inc.

President, Robert J. George
Editor-In-Chief, Robert Manning
Managing Editor, Paul Dreyfus
Marketing Director, Jeanne Gibson

Field Publications

President, Bruce H. Seide
Publisher, Marilyn Black
Marketing Director, Kathleen E. Long

Rizzoli Editore

Authors of the Italian Edition
  Introduction: Professor Ovidio Dallera
  Frederick the Great and Prussia: Professor Gherardo Bozzetti
  Napoleon and Europe: Dr. Flavio Conti
  Maps: Gian Franco Leonardi
Idea and Realization, Harry C. Lindinger
Graphic Design, Gerry Valsecchi
General Editorial Supervisor, Ovidio Dallera

© 1987 by Rizzoli Editore
Printed in the United States.

Library of Congress Catalog Card Number: 79-2528
ISBN: 0-15-004034-2

Field Publications offers handsome bookends and other decorative desk items. For information, write to:
Field Publications, P.O. Box 16617, Columbus, Ohio 43216.

Contents

Preface

During the Age of Enlightenment in the seventeenth and eighteenth centuries, traditions were subjected to the light of reason and often abandoned in favor of more efficient practices. Philosophers and publicists of the time believed that the monarch's role was to administer the state for the good of society. They hoped to see the "end of ideology" as effective government brought about universal well-being without extensive change; very few systematically opposed the social, political, or economic systems prevailing in Europe.

European monarchs were only too happy to centralize power and strengthen their governments at the expense of the feudal liberties of noble estates. Allying themselves with the Enlightenment's philosophes, they exposed the self-seeking nature of entrenched interests. They made conscientious attempts to advance learning, limit the role of the Church, introduce modern agricultural techniques, improve transportation, and stimulate industrial expansion. While Europe's bourgeoisie profited most visibly from these changes, the nobility and lower classes also benefited.

Yet the role of king was not disinterestedly technocratic, even if philosophes like Voltaire and Denis Diderot enthusiastically praised these "Enlightened Despots" for their constructive efforts (often receiving lavish presents from their royal friends). Monarchs remained close to the medieval view of the warrior-king who led his nobles into battle for glory—and not really far from the Baroque theory of divine right, which made the king answerable only to God for his deeds. Most rulers recoiled before the growth of the bourgeoisie and sought to secure their ties to the nobles by bestowing monopolies of high positions in the military and civil bureaucracies.

Two great rulers who represented both the technocratic and the arbitrary traditions of kingship were Frederick the Great of Prussia (1712–1786) and Napoleon Bonaparte of France (1769–1821). They shared a similar passion for the army and displayed remarkable military abilities that won them dominant positions in Europe. They also shared an unwavering devotion to long hours of official drudgery, overseeing every aspect of their rapidly growing administrations. Both men read widely, particularly in the practical literature applicable to day-to-day affairs: law, finance, trade, military science, and politics. Neither tolerated political opposition. The result was the creation of superb military machines amply supported by the full resources of the state. Both Frederick and Napoleon launched campaigns that brought glory to themselves and to the state—and untold misery to soldiers and taxpayers.

Differences as well as similarities can be discerned between the two. Frederick, on the one hand, came from a line of monarchs who ruled Brandenburg-Prussia for generations. As an adult, he was introverted and withdrawn, avoiding the capital, Berlin, in favor of his country residence. An aesthete, he was absorbed in musical pursuits—and apparently immune to human relationships. Napoleon, on the other hand, rose from impoverished Corsican nobility to become emperor of France and ruler of most of Europe. (The French Revolution of the late eighteenth century had so dislocated French society that new leaders like Napoleon could emerge. Yet France could not sustain a bourgeois republic for long and gradually restored a modified form of noble privilege and monarchical rule.) Unlike Frederick, Napoleon was showy, publicity-seeking, and emotional, heartily enjoying the pleasures of the imperial throne.

Cautious in the extreme, Frederick took only one great military risk—the conquest of Silesia in 1740—and devoted the rest of his long reign to protecting his acquisition. The partition of Poland in 1772, while ardently desired, came about almost by accident and only because of Russian and Austrian support. A skillful commander and diplomat, Frederick left Prussia stronger than he found it; he paved the way for Germany's rise to power a century later. In contrast, flamboyance, or perhaps the lack of a restraining family tradition, led Napoleon to take greater and greater risks until he finally invaded Russia and brought his empire to ruin. Reduced to its former borders, France was never again able to dominate Europe militarily.

Sober and practical in method but ambitious in aim, the Enlightened Despots enjoyed absolute power that they used to build or destroy their states according to whim and temperament.

DANIEL STONE
Professor of History
University of Winnipeg

Frederick the Great and Prussia

In the fall of 1740, the literary gossips of Europe had something to talk about. A publisher in The Hague had just brought out a book which refuted Machiavelli's *The Prince*, and it was an open secret that the anonymous author was a member of the royalty. A second edition appeared within weeks, altered and prefaced by its editor, Voltaire, France's most famous man of letters. By that time everyone knew that the author, whom Voltaire praised but never named, was the newly crowned king of Prussia, Frederick II, later hailed the Great. Voltaire called the book—and the king—*Antimachiavel*.

SANS, SOUCI.

Machiavelli, the celebrated political theorist of the Italian Renaissance, had claimed that a ruler is above ordinary morality, that he should be guided by only one principle—*raison d'état*, "reasons of state." Not so, contended *Antimachiavel*. Frederick argued that a ruler is not free to do just anything that works, and that reasons of state do not warrant all departures from the usual standards of virtue. According to the Prussian king, Machiavelli may be a serious political thinker but he simply "dismisses the most elementary principles of justice; he acknowledges only self-interest and violence." Point for point the book disputed Machiavelli's opportunism, printing *The Prince* in one column and Frederick's criticisms in the next.

The book was a sensation. In fifteen months, *Antimachiavel* went through sixteen editions, including translations. Voltaire, the "prince of philosophers," praised a new philosopher prince. "It is a happiness for the human race," he wrote, "that at last virtue has been ornamented more beautifully than vice." Rousseau ended the fifth book of his *Confessions* with the optimistic projection that the king "so short a time on his throne has already announced what in a short time more he will show himself to be."

In a short time more, however, the young king of Prussia showed himself to be something else alto-gether. A few days after Frederick's book was published, the last male Hapsburg emperor of Austria died. Questions about the succession left a power vacuum in central Europe, and Frederick responded with a classic Machiavellian land grab. In December of 1740, he ordered his superbly trained army into the rich and strategically valuable Austrian province of Silesia. What had become of Antimachiavel? He had broken Prussia's pledge to support the succession of the Austrian heir, Maria Theresa. He had launched an audacious, unprovoked attack on a peaceful neighbor. He had acquired a rich territory by a naked appeal to arms. He had seemed one thing and had been another. In all this he had but one justification—*raison d'état*, the greatness of Prussia. A disillusioned Voltaire remarked sardonically on "the victory of my good friend the king of Prussia, who wrote so well against Machiavel, and acted immediately like the heroes of Machiavel." Frederick and Voltaire exchanged angry letters, as the king halfheartedly tried to withdraw his book from publication and disingenuously renounced Voltaire's role in its development. Their friendship cooled—although not for the last time—and their correspondence was broken off for a while.

It is difficult to imagine how the Hohenzollerns, the

Tornow, a small Prussian town north of Berlin in a region now part of the German Democratic Republic (East Germany), included several vast estates (left). Until the East German government introduced agrarian reforms after World War Two, such estates formed the backbone of Prussian agriculture. The Junkers, or traditional land-owning nobility, hired large numbers of wage earners and farmers, many of them Polish immigrants, to work the land. The Junker estates have since been divided into family farms joined into collectives, on which cattle are raised and potatoes, beets, sugar, and rye are cultivated.

Prussia's former lands have been partitioned among neighboring countries. Portions of Prussia's old Baltic province of Pomerania (immediately below) now belong to East Germany; the remainder is Polish. Similarly, the adjacent region of Masuria (below left) comprises part of present-day Poland. The Riesengebirge, or Giant Mountains (bottom right), near the source of the Elbe River, were also once Prussian, but have since been absorbed by Poland and Czechoslovakia.

Far left, below, a view of the countryside in East Prussia, which since World War Two has been divided between Poland and the USSR. The horses in the foreground are a prize breed from Trakehnen (east of Königsberg), an area celebrated for its steeds since 1732, when Frederick William I began housing the royal stud there.

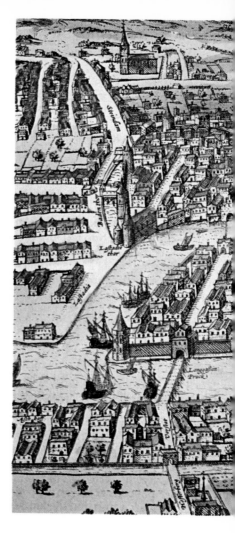

Above, Frederick William, the Great Elector of Brandenburg from 1640 to 1688, with his consort Louisa Henrietta of Orange-Nassau and their three children, including the future King Frederick I of Prussia (at right).

The Prussian Hohenzollerns originally came from southwestern Germany, where by the tenth century the family had built its ancestral castle (below) on a site not far from Sigmaringen.

German royal family that was Frederick's dynasty, could have accomplished what they did without a heavy dose of Machiavellianism. What they managed, in the relatively short span of two and a quarter centuries, was to transform a weak north German princedom into the nucleus of the German Empire, whose leader was a Hohenzollern.

Frederick the Great's predecessors confronted a formidable array of problems, stemming first from geography. In the mid-seventeenth century, the margrave elector of bleak Brandenburg—often called "the sandbox of Germany"—in the northeast corner of the Holy Roman Empire, also held the title of duke of Prussia, an impoverished enclave on the Baltic shores beyond the empire's eastern boundaries. (Originally conquered by the medieval monastic knights of the Teutonic Order, Prussia passed to secular and Lutheran rule under the order's last grand master, the Hohenzollern Prince Albrecht of Brandenburg, in 1525.) The margrave elector inherited still other Hohenzollern lands, most of them tiny provinces scattered from the banks of Switzerland's Lake Geneva (Lac Léman) through southern and central Germany to the Lower Rhine. None of these territories had defensible borders. None was rich, strategically located, or populous. None had strong ties with the

MONS REGIVS; PRVSSIÆ,
SIVE BORVSSIÆ, VRBS
MARITIMA, ELEGANTIS:
SIMA PRINCIPIS SEDES.

others except through a common prince. The Hohenzollerns presided over a most confused and motley realm.

These diverse lands were surrounded by powerful, ambitious neighbors. To the north, Sweden had long controlled the Baltic. In the early 1600s, Sweden's armies had ravaged Germany in battles with the Holy Roman emperor. To the west, France under Louis XIV had grown to be the greatest European military power of the remainder of the century. Eastward lay a large if unstable Poland, whose territory separated Brandenburg from Prussia. Beyond was Russia, now beginning ominously to turn its attention toward Europe. To the south lay Austria, Hungary, and other lands of the Hapsburgs, who added prestige to their power by wearing the crown of the Holy Roman emperor. These were Europe's great powers, and in their diplomatic, religious, and military rivalries Brandenburg-Prussia was often in the middle of the board, and sometimes expendable.

The Hohenzollern princes also had to cope with diverse political attachments. Brandenburg itself was part of the Holy Roman Empire, and its margrave was a subject of the Holy Roman emperor, whose real power came not from his imperial dignity but from his Hapsburg family possessions, especially Austria,

This sixteenth-century print (above) depicts the East Prussian capital of Königsberg. Founded in 1255, Königsberg was dominated by a fortress of the Teutonic Knights and from 1525 to 1618 served as the residence of the dukes of Prussia. Now part of the Soviet Union, the city was renamed Kaliningrad in 1946. Below, a castle in Marienburg, once an East Prussian city and today—renamed Malbork—part of Poland. Marienburg was the site of the famous 1656 treaty that sealed an alliance between Frederick William and Charles X Gustavus, king of Sweden. By the next year, though, the union had dissolved.

Moravia, and Hungary. Within the confederation of princely German states called the Holy Roman Empire, the Hohenzollern ruler of Brandenburg was one of the seven prince electors, holding the right to vote for a new Holy Roman emperor. To complicate matters further, Prussia was not even part of the empire; until 1660 its ruler was vassal to the king of Poland, and thereafter an independent prince.

Even within Brandenburg-Prussia, the prince's authority was restricted. He was forced to share power with firmly entrenched local authorities, who zealously guarded their ancient customs. The proud Junkers, or rural nobility, and the city councils habitually challenged the ruler's right to tax, to raise an army, or to regulate trade. The nobles and other traditionally privileged groups were considered the "estates" of Brandenburg-Prussia just as the elector and his fellow princes were considered the "estates" of the Holy Roman Empire. In each case the rules of feudalism required the ruler—be he emperor or prince—to share political responsibility with his estates.

The wonder is that Frederick the Great, building on the accomplishments of his remarkable family, actually made his unlikely realm into one of the great powers of Europe. A century before his accession, Brandenburg-Prussia was disunited, poor, and beleaguered; less than a century after his death, it had created Germany's Second Reich, or Empire. Perhaps the feat would have been impossible if Frederick had relied solely upon the theoretical idealism of Antimachiavel. To ensure the success of his mission he also made consummate use of the practical realism advocated by Machiavelli.

If he needed any lessons in Machiavellianism he had only to study the career of his great-grandfather Frederick William. This extraordinary Hohenzollern, who put Prussia on the road to greatness, was known even in his own lifetime as the Great Elector. He became the margrave elector of Brandenburg and duke of Prussia in 1640, just one hundred years before his scion published Antimachiavel.

At the time, Germany was being ravaged by the

In 1675, Frederick William, the Great Elector, defeated the formidable Swedes, his former allies, in the battle of Fehrbellin. This triumph of Prussian arms, shown at left in an old Dutch print, helped the elector tighten his control over the Prussian state, which trebled in territory during his lifetime. A standing army, Prussia's first, justified new taxes and helped Frederick William dominate the towns and rural nobility.

Frederick William the Great Elector (above) appears with his triumphant officers after the conquest of Wolgast. This northern Pomeranian town commanded access to the Stettiner Haff, a vast lagoon separated from the Baltic only by a chain of sandy islands. Access to the sea was an important goal of the Great Elector's mercantilist policy, which led him to build a fleet (left) based in the Baltic.

Right, a modern view of Fehrbellin, a small town just northwest of Berlin in present-day East Germany. Here, in one of the great battles of the seventeenth century, Prussian armies routed mighty Sweden, demonstrating the effectiveness of the Great Elector's domestic reorganization. Frederick's new taxes, levied on everything from land to beer, financed a well-trained permanent army—an improvement over undisciplined mercenary troops. He was responsible for building a force of thirty thousand men, an unprecedented achievement in Germany.

When the Great Elector died in 1688, his son Frederick became Elector Frederick III. Shortly after succeeding his father, he began supplying troops to the Imperial army. Thus beholden to Frederick for his military backing, the Holy Roman emperor eventually yielded to Frederick's long-standing request for a royal title. In elaborate ceremonies at Königsberg in January 1701, the elector crowned himself Frederick I (left), king in Prussia.

Below, a scene from an opera-ballet produced in Hamburg to celebrate the coronation of Frederick I. Right, the new king's triumphal entry into Berlin in 1701. Frederick I made Berlin his royal capital that year, and it soon became one of Europe's great cities.

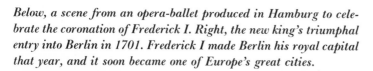

Thirty Years' War (1618–1648)—that last great religious conflict in a century and a half of religious tension. The fighting left Brandenburg decimated. Many villages were divested of surviving adult males. Crops went unplanted, the population was starving, and epidemics were rampant. The government was in shambles, and the Swedish army occupied many of the Hohenzollern principalities in northern Germany.

Brandenburg's internal affairs were run largely by a powerful war minister, Adam von Schwartzenberg. A Catholic, Schwartzenberg had placed the army of Protestant Brandenburg-Prussia under oath to the Catholic Holy Roman Empire during the Thirty Years' War. This largely mercenary army had tried unsuccessfully to wrest the neighboring province of Pomerania on the Baltic coast from the Swedes and then began to harass the people of Brandenburg.

The Europe of 1650 was a dangerous place for small states. In the aftermath of the Thirty Years' War, a few great powers had emerged on the international scene, and although religious passions had cooled, the equally bellicose dynastic ambitions of these nations remained. In the west, France was envious of the new wealth and commercial prowess of the Netherlands; it also continued its centuries-old ri-

ralry with Austria. To the east, Poland, weakened by constitutional deficiencies and a squabbling nobility, became a tempting prey for Sweden and Russia—a prey uncomfortably close to Prussia. Russia, under Peter the Great, was emerging from centuries of backwardness and ethnocentricism, and would soon seek its fortunes in Europe.

Amid these domestic and foreign perils, the Great Elector was governed by Machiavelli's maxim—*raison d'état*. Whatever policy effectively increased the power and prestige of Prussia and its prince was the policy to be followed. At times, that meant supporting the Protestant powers of Europe against Catholic France

and Poland. The prince's personal preferences as well inclined him toward the Protestants. Having been educated by gifted Calvinist tutors in the Dutch court of William of Orange, Frederick William remained a fervent Protestant all his life. Yet when Prussia's interests were involved he did not hesitate to fight shoulder to shoulder with the Catholics against his coreligionists. Frederick William's desire for a seacoast, for example, pitted him repeatedly against the Protestant Swedes.

Through all the confusing twists of his career, his ambition for advancing Prussia's greatness never faltered. One of the most important steps to this end was to gain authority over taxation. Before the time of Frederick William, the elector's real power was limited to two narrow functions of government: the handling of certain lawsuits, mostly on appeal, and a responsibility, at least theoretically, for foreign policy. He could levy no direct taxes, and indirect ones, politely called "contributions," could be created only in time of war and with the consent of the estates. He could raise an army only by begging troops from the noblemen. His sole direct source of wealth was the land he owned as a Junker. Without independent regulation of state finances, the elector could never control the army, and without an army he would be unable to pursue his goals in foreign policy.

The Great Elector set out to build a strong army backed by independent financing. "Alliances, to be sure, are good," he once said, "but a force of one's own, on which one can rely, is better. A ruler is treated with no consideration if he does not have troops and means of his own. It is these that have made me *considérable* since the time when I began to have them." The Great Elector began enlisting the help of the estates in sacking his war minister, Schwartzenberg, and in putting the army under oath to himself. Then he sought new ways of raising money and troops, directly challenging the traditional rights of the estates to form an army.

The result was a fundamental change in the constitution of Brandenburg-Prussia. For the first time a standing army under the elector's direct control and a tax-collecting civil service to pay for it emerged. The Junkers were allowed a free hand on their own domains, but province-wide political authority, based on the army and bureaucracy, was concentrated in the hands of the elector as never before. In addition, the income of the state tripled, and the size of the peacetime army increased more than fifteen-fold.

Frederick William used his newly centralized power adroitly on the chessboard of European politics. During the Great Northern War (1655–1660), which pitted Sweden against Poland, the Great Elector turned from one side to the other with such deftness that Prussia came out ahead every time. First he sided with Sweden's great warrior king, Charles X Gustavus, and helped with the bloody battle of Warsaw in 1656, alerting Europeans to Prussia's emergent military strength. The next year, however, the Great Elector nimbly abandoned his ally to fight for the Poles, then extracted his price: The Polish king was forced to relinquish his claim to suzerainty over East Prussia. The Prussians also conquered Swedish Pomerania and acquired a long-coveted seacoast—which they later lost at the conference table at the war's end in 1660.

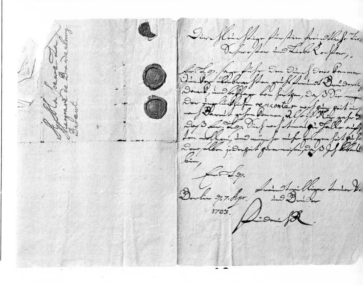

Frederick I (right) chose Lietzenburg, then on Berlin's outskirts, as the site for a new palace, which was named Charlottenburg for his second wife. The exterior (above) and the royal study (left) were extensively restored after Charlottenburg burned during the bombings of Berlin in 1943. The palace is now a museum and houses many valuable works of art.

Below left, a letter written by Frederick I, bearing the royal seal. Sophia Charlotte of Hanover (below) was the second of Frederick's three wives and mother of his heir, Frederick William I.

The Prussian prince got another chance to gain a coastline in 1672. In that year, France's Louis XIV invaded the Netherlands, starting the Dutch War (1672–1678), and as usual Frederick William played both ends against the middle. First he sided with the Dutch. But when the Holy Roman emperor finally mobilized Germany against the French, the elector refused to participate, making a separate peace with France rather than share the defense of German soil with the emperor. From Vienna, the philosopher Leibnitz, who was acting as an adviser to the Holy Roman emperor, likened Frederick to Achilles, sulking in his tents. Brandenburg-Prussia was back in the anti-French alliance a few months later, however, and its troops fought splendidly in Alsace until Sweden, France's former ally, invaded Brandenburg. Frederick William's ambition returned: If the Swedes could be defeated, Pomerania might be made Prussian. In a string of brilliantly fought, fast-moving battles, they were indeed conquered, most resoundingly at Fehrbellin, a triumph that greatly enhanced

the reputation of Prussian arms. But once again, as i 1660, the gains of the battlefield were lost at the con ference table. At the peace of 1679, Pomerania wa returned to Sweden.

Brandenburg-Prussia was now emerging as power in Europe, but not yet a great power. That wa partly because it was still subject to the overlordshi of the Holy Roman emperor, who refused to proclair the Brandenburg rulers king. The prestige of kingshi had enormous import in late seventeenth-centur Europe. Louis XIV, who dazzled the continent wit the splendor of Versailles, epitomized the glories tha accompanied a royal title. More important, the Su King demonstrated how a king could break the powe of his nobility and gather absolute power in hi hands. Princes all over Europe learned French, ape the court ceremony of Versailles, and longed to b absolute monarchs like Louis. The Great Elector use France as a model for many of his innovations, in cluding much that later was seen as archetypicall

Above, the dignified castle of the dukes of Pomerania, in the city of Stettin. Long a Swedish possession, Stettin was ceded to Prussia in 1720. Far left, Prussia's Frederick William I (reigned 1713–1740).

Frederick William I's queen (near left), Sophia Dorothea, receives Augustus II, the Strong, of Saxony and Poland. Below, a short letter in German penned in the hand of Frederick William I.

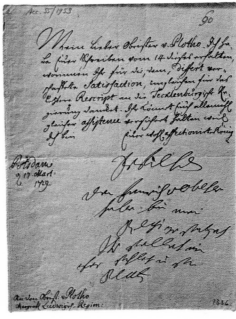

Frederick William, the Great Elector, initiated a Hohenzollern tradition by welcoming persecuted French Huguenots to sparsely populated Prussia. Many later immigrants to the region, including oppressed Jews and German Protestants, made important contributions to Prussia's commercial, industrial, and agricultural development. In this allegorical print (left) a family of Protestant peasants leaves Salzburg, Austria, to seek the protection of the Prussian king.

Although Frederick William I introduced compulsory education to Prussia in 1717, schools did not thrive. The teachers were often former soldiers and moonlighting craftsmen, hired by a king who was more interested in military training than in cultural pursuits. In this painting (above) of his visit to an elementary school, Frederick's nonchalant posture and the inattention of his officers convey the indifferent quality of Prussia's early educational system.

As an old man, Frederick William I took up painting to distract himself from the painful degenerative disease of which he eventually died. His undistinguished paintings are almost all of military subjects. In this portrait (right), the king is shown at his easel; a soldier stands guard in the background. Left, the Sergeant King with one of his beloved Prussian grenadiers. The people called this elite Potsdam unit of soldiers Longshanks, and viewed them with a mixture of humor and wonder, as the playful parody in this contemporary popular print suggests.

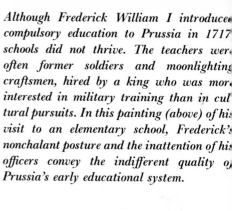

"Prussian"—a rigid bureaucratic control of the economy, an aggressive foreign policy, pompous court ritual, and, above all, militarism.

In 1688, Frederick William's son succeeded the Great Elector as Elector Frederick III of Brandenburg and duke of Prussia. He was a loyal ally of the Holy Roman emperor during the generation-long string of wars that the aging Louis XIV began in the year of the Great Elector's death. But Frederick III had an ulterior motive for his loyalty, based on his longing for a royal title: Only the Holy Roman emperor could recognize Frederick as king. The elector besieged his overlord with gifts, flattery, and petitions—and bore with humiliating refusals. At last he showed he could be clever as well as a sycophant. In 1700, with the War of the Spanish Succession on the horizon, in which Germany would be pitted against France, Frederick threatened to withhold troops from the army of Holy Roman Emperor Leopold I unless the emperor allowed him a royal title. The reluctant Leopold finessed the question by permitting Frederick to style himself "king in Prussia." Prussia lay outside the Holy Roman Empire, and if Frederick was not king *of* it, but only *in* it, he would seem less threatening to—and more dependent on—his imperial lord.

That arrangement was good enough for the elector. He promptly traveled to the Prussian capital of Königsberg (now Kaliningrad, USSR) and with great pomp crowned himself Frederick I, king in Prussia. Years later, Frederick's grandson and namesake, King Frederick II, the Great, wrote that "what originally was a case of vanity later turned out to be a masterpiece of politics. The royal title freed the house of Brandenburg. . . . It was a bait which Frederick III threw out to his descendants, as if to say: 'I have gained a title, now make yourselves worthy of it.'"

After becoming a king, Frederick I slyly began to transfer his royal dignity from Königsberg to his most important province, Brandenburg, in the Holy Roman Empire. In the year of his coronation, 1701, he moved his capital to Berlin, and his territories, including Brandenburg, soon came to be known as Prussia. The old Baltic province of Prussia, to the east of Pomerania, was named "East Prussia." The emperor quickly discovered that a legalistic distinction between "in" and "of" would not prevent the Hohenzollern king from exhibiting his newly acquired claim to royalty.

Frederick's acquisition of the royal title complemented his love of pomp and display. He hired the gifted architect Andreas Schlüter to design ornate Baroque palaces near Berlin and in Charlottenburg. He also built the University of Halle, and under the influence of his wife, Queen Sophia Charlotte, and

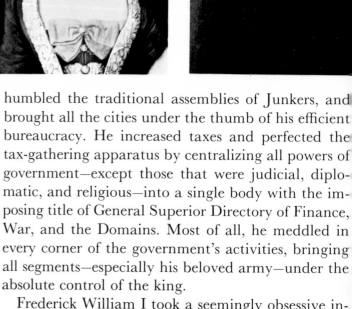

A contemporary print (above) shows King Frederick William I drawing his sword in a fury against his son Frederick, as an officer intervenes.

In 1733 the king forced Crown Prince Frederick to marry the rather uninspiring Princess Elisabeth Christine of Brunswick (below).

Right, Wilhelmina of Prussia, the eldest child of Frederick William I and favorite sister of Frederick II, the Great. She and Frederick shared a forlorn childhood, tyrannized by their brutal martinet of a father. Frederick always confided in his sister, even after she married the margrave of Ansbach-Bayreuth. Their correspondence is among the most interesting to survive from the eighteenth century.

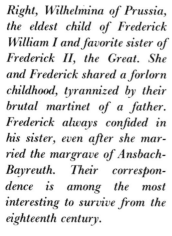

her friend Leibnitz, the great philosopher and mathematician, Frederick founded the Berlin Academy of Sciences to glorify his realm. In the world of politics, Frederick I realized the long-standing goal of annexing Pomerania, but otherwise merely maintained the power his father had accrued. He was neither a great war captain nor a brilliant diplomat. And it was only after his death in 1713 that Prussia underwent as vigorous a program of nation-building as the one carried out under Frederick William.

Frederick I's son and successor, King Frederick William I, was a worthy namesake of the Great Elector and the true founder of the Prussian state. He

humbled the traditional assemblies of Junkers, and brought all the cities under the thumb of his efficient bureaucracy. He increased taxes and perfected the tax-gathering apparatus by centralizing all powers of government—except those that were judicial, diplomatic, and religious—into a single body with the imposing title of General Superior Directory of Finance, War, and the Domains. Most of all, he meddled in every corner of the government's activities, bringing all segments—especially his beloved army—under the absolute control of the king.

Frederick William I took a seemingly obsessive interest in his soldiers. He was particularly devoted to a

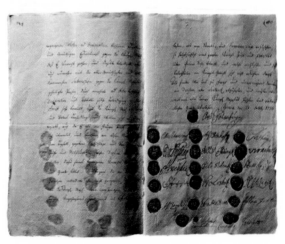

Center, a portrait of the crown prince of Prussia before his accession as King Frederick II, later hailed the Great. His father, Frederick William I, was shocked by his son's attempt to flee Prussia in 1730—an act for which the prince and two friends were convicted of desertion, with his companions condemned to death. The death sentence (left) was carried out against only one of his accomplices. Later, Frederick was to live quietly with his wife in Rheinsberg Castle (above).

pecial guard at Potsdam, composed entirely of enormously tall men recruited and even kidnaped from all over Europe to serve the king. The people nicknamed them Longshanks—and Frederick William, the Sergeant King. Under him the Prussian army established its tradition of perfect drill, robotlike obedience, and flawless discipline.

Frederick William I thus built the Prussian state on the twin foundations laid by the Great Elector—the army and the bureaucracy. It was a matter of highest importance for Prussia, and for Germany as a whole, that these two institutions embody the typically Prussian virtue of obedience. As a nation of soldiers and officials, Prussia valued order and authority above freedom and consensus.

To Frederick William I, discipline was as much a private virtue as a state goal. He worked—and often behaved—like a demon. The king was a coarse, graceless man who had no pleasures aside from boisterous parties and occasional hunting trips. He was a tyrant to his family, whom he confined to a few rooms of the palace. The rest of the royal residence was occupied by bureaucrats who were watched vigilantly and by soldiers who trained on gardens that had been transformed into drill grounds.

Tobacco

Snuff-taking—the inhaling of pulverized, aromatic tobacco leaves—was a mark of refinement and elegance in the eighteenth century, and snuffboxes, often made with gold and silver and studded with precious gems, were regarded as objets d'art. Typically, these diminutive boxes depicted scenes ranging from tiny portraits of royalty through the stock motifs of classical myth and conventional gallantry to erotic themes. The more elegant snuffboxes acquired a conspicuous place in court ritual and diplomacy, where they served as useful gifts and, occasionally, tasteful bribes.

The famous Tobacco Society of the Prussian court was founded by the style-conscious Frederick I, whose son, Frederick William I, turned it into a crude, stag smoking club and informal privy council. Frederick William's son, Frederick the Great, preferred the more genteel snuff to a pipe, and indulged a passion for valuable snuffboxes; some observers estimated that he had no fewer than 1,500 in his private collection.

Right, Frederick William I (second from right at table) with members of his Tobacco Society. Just beyond the king is young Frederick, who was offended by such coarse gatherings. The club had been founded for the decorous enjoyment of the new fad of smoking, but under Frederick William I, vast quantities of beer appeared along with the delicate Dutch clay pipes, and the meetings inevitably became boisterous and vulgar.

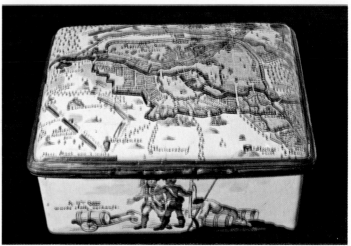

Fashionable, elaborately decorated snuffboxes were often exchanged among royalty. Five boxes from Frederick the Great's extensive collection depict (clockwise from top right) the names of famous Prussian victories during the Seven Years' War (1756–1763); Russian armies entering Berlin during the same war; a sleeping huntsman (in a diamond-encrusted box); the Roman woodland goddess, Diana, at her bath; and Frederick, in a miniature.

As sometimes happens, this unpleasant man had a son utterly unlike himself, except in strength of will. The crown prince Frederick lived his whole boyhood in conflict with his father. At the age of seven he was taken from his beloved governesses and delivered over to officers who tutored him. The king prescribed every detail of his day, from a six o'clock rising through specified prayers, grooming, and breakfast, and then studies, mostly history and catechism. But Frederick also contrived to learn Latin and the classics, as well as French literature and culture. The boy grew to love the wit, irreverence, and rational elegance of the French Enlightenment, and as he matured he developed tastes that his father abhorred. He learned to play the flute and came to adore Italian music. He turned from his father's stern Protestantism to a skeptical deism. He became withdrawn and haughty, and cultivated an ironic disdain for his father's court.

Conflict between father and son was often violent. Frederick William regularly beat the crown prince. At mealtimes he made a practice of throwing soup—plate and all—at his son. Wilhelmina, Frederick's adoring sister, wrote in her memoirs that the king once would have strangled him if a page had not intervened.

Matters came to a head in 1730, when Frederick was eighteen. England had proposed that Anglo-Prussian ties be strengthened by a marriage between Frederick and the English princess Amelia. The idea delighted Frederick's mother, Queen Sophia Dorothea, as she was the sister of England's King George II. But King Frederick William I was not so sure of the benefits of this marriage. What influence might this elegant and probably sinful English princess have on the wayward Fritz?

While the king was clumsily negotiating with the English, Frederick acted. In the company of his closest friend, Lieutenant Hans Herman von Katte, he fled the court for England. His plans were disclosed, however, and the pair was caught. The king was furious. Both youths, being soldiers, were court-martialed for desertion; Frederick was imprisoned and Katte condemned to death. Another friend escaped but was condemned *in absentia*. A scaffold was erected on a level with Frederick's cell window, and one gray November morning the crown prince was forced to watch while Katte was beheaded. By royal order, the body was left on the scaffold in full view all day.

The tragedy had a grim effect on the young crown prince. He withdrew into himself. His prison sentence in the provincial city of Küstrin (now Kostrzyn, Po-

The year 1740 saw the death of two important German rulers—the king of Prussia and the emperor of Austria. Frederick II, the new Prussian king (painted at left while still a crown prince; reigned 1740–1786), immediately opened hostilities against the Austrian heiress Maria Theresa (above).

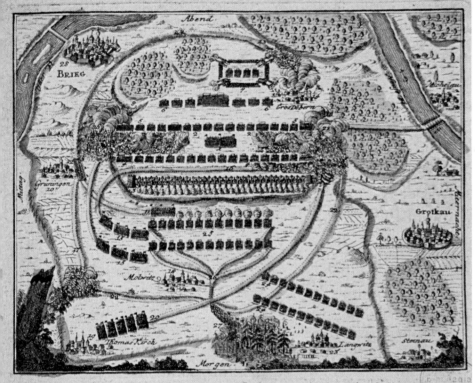

Eigentliche Abbildung und wahre Vorstellung des Lagers und
scharssen Gefechts; welches zwischen der Preußischen und Oesterreichischen
Armee An. 1741. den 10. April bey Molwitz zwischen Brieg und Ohlau,
in Schlesien vorgegangen.

Above, the ensign of a Hungarian infantry regiment in Maria Theresa's army. Her forces lost the first battle of her reign, fought in April 1741 at Mollwitz in Lower Silesia, to Prussia. The Prussian victory (left, from the Act of Annexation of Silesia) was so uncertain, however, that Frederick fled the field before witnessing the outcome, believing the day was lost.

N. 1. der Ort und die Stelle wo sich der König biß zum Angriff befunden. 2. Die Königliche Leib-Garde welche vieles Lob verdienet, ihrer Tapferkeit halben. 3. Die Preußische Artillerie von viertel und halben Carthaunen auch Geschwind-Stücken. 4. Das vordere Treffen. 5. Das mittlere Treffen. 6. Das hintere Treffen. 7. Die Wagenburg. 8. Morästige Gräben, welche den Feinde eine Falle waren, und von den Preußen mit Schnee zugedecket worden sind. 9. Die Schiff-Brücke worüber die Preußische Armee paßiret. 10. Hierinnen hatten die Oesterreichischen Husaren ihr Quartier. 11. Ruckten die Husaren aus dem Dorfe und stellten sich gegen die Preußen in die Fronte. 12. Da die Husaren der Preußen Lunten rochen, ergaben sie sich auf Flucht, und fasten bey ihrem Quartier Posto. 13. Wie die Husaren unter währendem Treffen sich hinunter ziehen, in die Bagage einfallen, und grossen Schaden machen. 14. Das Dorf, so die Husaren unter währender Action geplündert, und in Brand gestecket. 15. Die 6. Oesterreichischen Regimenter Cavallerie vom rechten Flügel, welche, weilen niemand vorhanden, ein dreymaliges General-Salve aushielten, und durch der Preußen Eindringen den lincken Flügel ausmachten. 16. Der heldenmüthige und sehr tapfere Angriff der Cavallerie, unter Anführung des Herrn General-Feld-Marschall-Lieutenants, Baron von Römer, wie sie der Preußen rechten Flügel attaquiren, auch etliche Stücke erbeutet, und sie wider die Feinde brauchten, deren Reuterey zu Grunde richteten, biß auf den lincken Flügel verfolgten, und bis an die Stelle des Königs drungen, doch aber von der Königl. Leib-Garde zurück geschlagen, und sich zu retiriren gezwungen wurden. 17. Wie sich die Cavallerie durch das immerwährende Feuer der Preußen zurück ziehet, und gegen Neiß unter die Stücke begiebet. 18. Haupt-Quartier der 6. Regimenter vom rechten Flügel, unter Herrn General Römer, als Althan, Seher, Hohenembs, Römer, Lanthieri, Birckenfeld. 19. Das Quartier der andern 5. Regimenter Cavallerie auf den lincken Flügel, nemlich: Lichtenstein, Cordua, Bathiani, Zollnern und Alt-Würtemberg. 20. Der 5. Regimenter Cavallerie vom lincken Flügel Anmarsch. 21. Der ungemeine Angriff und glückliche Attaque der 5. Regimenter vom lincken Flügel, unter Anführung des Hrn. General-Feld-Marschall-Lieut. Baron von Berlichingen. 22. Wie sich die Oesterreichische Cavallerie zu retiriren genöthiget siehet, und von den Preußen unter vielen Blut-Vergiessen gegen Neiß zu, wendet. 23. Das Quartier, wo die Oesterreichische Infanterie und Artillerie lag. 24. Der sämtlichen Infanterie und Artillerie schneller Anmarsch gegen die Preußen. 25. Die Stellung und der Ort wo die Oesterreichische Infanterie und Artillerie zu fechten anfieng. 26. Wie sie durch der Preußen unzertrennlich geschlossene Glieder, und erschröckliches Feuer, welches, wie ein immerwährendes Donner-Wetter war, sich retiriren musten. 27. Der Wald, wo sich die Oesterreichischen Völcker zu verbergen trachten, da hingegen die Königlich-Preußische Armee auf der Seite stehend geblieben, und den andern Tag Grotkau und andere Städte wiederum besetzet hat. 28. Darauf die Vestung Brieg berennet, und zur Übergabe aufgefordert. Der preißwürdigste König, welcher einen ungemeinen Helden-Muth bewiesen hat, ohngeachtet etliche Kugeln vom Cuiraß abgesprungen, dennoch jederzeit in dem grösten und stärckesten Feuer sich finden lassen, auch bey Weichung seines rechten Flügels, ihnen zugeruffen: Ihr Brüder und Kinder, rettet doch der Preussen Ehre, und euers Königs Leben; welches auch so viel gefruchtet, daß die Preußische Armee nicht nur desperat gefochten, sondern auch die Oesterreichischen Völcker glücklich aus dem Feld geschlagen.

Bottom left, a sketch of troop deployment for the battle of Mollwitz, drawn by Frederick and sent in a letter to Prince Leopold I of Anhalt-Dessau. Below, a Prussian infantry helmet from the War of the Austrian Succession (1740–1748). Frederick took great pride in his army, the backbone of his power.

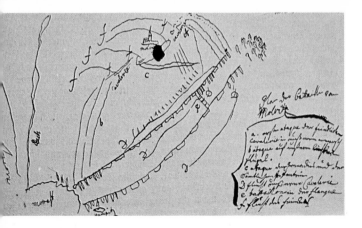

Prussian military uniforms

Prussia was renowned for its splendid army. Dressed in "Prussian blue" uniforms, the troops of Frederick William I dazzled Europe with their precise execution of military drills. Yet the Sergeant King's army was built on reputation alone, proving its true mettle only under its next commander, Frederick the Great.

Austria, too, had a glorious military tradition, but its army was less cohesive than that of Prussia. Drawn from all over the Hapsburg realms, and lacking a caste of officers, it relied on the tactical skill of its commanders, which was often insufficient to bring victory over the efficient Prussians.

Even Prussian civilian officials, such as this member of the staff of the Prussian royal stables (above), wore uniforms. The organization of the Prussian bureaucracy was markedly militaristic from the time of Frederick William, the Great Elector, onward.

Left, an officer and a soldier of the Fourth Prussian Regiment of Hussars. Hussars, or light cavalry, were a Hungarian innovation adopted in Prussia by Frederick the Great, who had two special regiments of these "death troops" under his command.

Prussian uniforms were greatly admired in Europe. The panel at left is reproduced from a tablet belonging to Landgrave Louis IX of Hesse-Darmstadt and shows uniforms of the Twelfth Regiment of Prussian Infantry. From left: a sergeant, a private, and a corporal of the grenadiers; and a noncommissioned officer and a private of the rifle corps. Grenadiers were prestigious troops who fought on foot, flanking the regular riflemen. Below, an infantry officer of the Fusilier Regiment of Prince Frederick Francis of Brunswick, an elite unit in the army of Frederick the Great.

After Maria Theresa's losses during the War of the Austrian Succession, she completely reorganized her army, borrowing many ideas from her enemy Frederick the Great. By the time of her death, the Austrian military force matched the Prussian army in size. From far left, seven eighteenth-century members of Austria's military: an artilleryman, two dragoons (heavily armed soldiers), a rifleman from a regiment from Friuli (a Lombard duchy), another artilleryman, a rifleman from the Regiment of the Prince of Hildburghausen, and a hussar of the Katnocky Regiment. Right, uniforms of officers from Prussia's Second Regiment of Hussars.

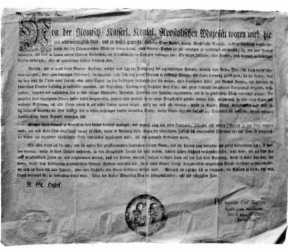

Desertion was a persistent problem plaguing eighteenth-century mercenary armies. A proclamation (left) from Maria Theresa announces amnesty for Austrian deserters. Below, a painting of the siege of Prague in 1742. Although Maria Theresa's troops withstood this siege, the city fell to Frederick the Great in 1744.

All of the Hohenzollern kings enlarged Prussia's domains, through either military conquest or clever diplomacy. Right, views of three cities that Prussia seized during the eighteenth century. Top to bottom: the castle at the Silesian town of Pless (present-day Pszczyna, Poland), which passed into Prussian hands during the War of the Austrian Succession; the university at Breslau (now Wrocław, Poland), where the preliminary treaty ceding Silesia to Prussia was signed in 1742; the cathedral at Poznań, a Polish city named Posen in German after Prussia acquired it in 1793 during the second partition of Poland.

land) was eventually commuted to exile, and by the king's order he was put to work as a clerk in the bureaucracy. When some time had passed he wrote an abject letter to his father begging for forgiveness. The king forced Frederick to marry a plain, dull princess from Brunswick and grudgingly gave him a household and a regiment in another provincial town, Rheinsberg. There the prince discreetly resumed his literary and artistic interests. The flute reappeared, and so did the French literature. He became a keen observer of the European political and military scene. He wrote *Antimachiavel*.

In the late spring of 1740 Frederick William I died, and Frederick was crowned King Frederick II. All the omens pointed to a reign of peace, culture, and tolerance. Was not the new king an anti-Machiavellian? And had he not dedicated his reign "to Apollo and the muses," as inscribed on the new Berlin Opera House? Was not that symbol of militarism, the Potsdam guard of Longshanks, dissolved?

But Frederick William I's efficient organization of the state was left unchanged, and everything remained under the king's direct control. Seven new regiments were added to the army. And just months after Frederick II took the throne, when Holy Roman Emperor Charles VI of Hapsburg died, leaving Maria Theresa as the sole heir, Frederick's crack Prussian troops invaded the Hapsburg province of Silesia.

The legal basis of Frederick's claim to Silesia was flimsy; he invaded this mineral-rich land simply because it was vulnerable and close at hand, its ruler weak, and the international scene confused. In short, he acted for Machiavellian "reasons of state." Frederick II then disingenuously agreed to honor his father's pledge to support the Pragmatic Sanction, Charles VI's plan for Maria Theresa's succession to the Hapsburg throne—but only if Maria Theresa would let him keep Silesia. Maria Theresa would not.

And so it came to war—the War of the Austrian Succession—which began badly for Frederick in April of 1741 at the battle of Mollwitz, where the king narrowly escaped capture. Although Britain backed Maria Theresa, its help was chiefly in the form of good advice and money. Frederick found an ally in Britain's archenemy France, as well as in Saxony and Bavaria, whose ruler hoped to become the Holy Roman emperor.

Frederick won his first real victory in the spring of 1742, at Chotusitz (now Chotusice, Czechoslovakia), but he began to worry about the price of success. If he and his French allies completely defeated Austria, France might come to dominate Germany and threaten Prussia. Frederick wanted an Austria that was weakened but not too weak. So by turns he with-

Above left, Frederick the Great with hi
nephew, whose play had interrupted th
king's work. When Frederick confiscated th
child's ball, the boy amused his uncle with hi
bravado in demanding it back. Above, Fred
erick visiting an agricultural colony.

Prussian soldiers (left) who had waited to
lodge a complaint respond with legendary
discipline when Frederick orders an about-
face; they simply march away unheard. The
artist, Peter Haas, executed an entire series
on the life of Frederick.

Frederick the Great considered himself the
first servant of the state, and he went out of
his way to maintain contact with ordinary
citizens. When riding in Potsdam (right), he
encountered a baker and a peasant arguing
over two sacks of grain. The king adjudicated
the dispute on the spot. Such examples of a
ruler's personal intervention in the details of
administration were no substitute for the
constitutional guarantees that Prussia
shunned.

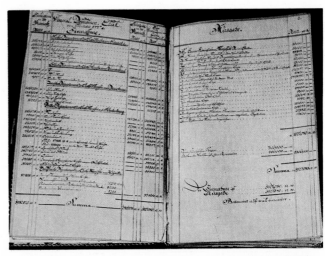

...ederick the Great kept meticulous written records of ...blic expenditures. Above right, a page of the State Accounts Book written in his own hand. Frederick was in...ested in industrializing his largely agricultural ...untry, as his sponsorship of the Baruth iron foundries ...ight) attests.

...rew from the war, re-entered it, and again withdrew. ...evitably, though, his very nimbleness imperiled his ...osition, for his erstwhile French allies learned to ...istrust him. In 1745 he took to the field for the last ...me. In two brilliant victories, at Hohenfriedeberg ...nd Soor, he outmaneuvered the Austrians and their ...llies, and on Christmas Day, 1745, Prussia and Aus-...ia finally made peace. Maria Theresa retained her ...arone, but Frederick kept Silesia. When he returned ...o Berlin, his subjects lauded him as Frederick the ...reat. Antimachiavel had proved himself a splendid ...Iachiavellian.

Frederick could now return to the cultured plea-...ares of his court life. He had moved to his new Ro-...oco palace near Potsdam, called Sanssouci, French ...or "without care." Modeled after Louis XIV's Ver-...ailles, it served as an eastern outpost of French cul-...ure and civilization, for this Prussian king had no use ...or things German. The very architecture of Sans-...ouci exudes a French influence.

At the palace, Frederick surrounded himself with ...earned Frenchmen, as well as Italians, Scots, and ...thers who shared the classical French attributes of ...it and clarity of thought and who could hold forth ...n the king's favorite philosophical inquiries. Musi-...ians were also welcomed to perform for, and with,

him. In 1747, Frederick hosted the aging Johann Se-bastian Bach, who wrote the *Musical Offering* for him, employing themes composed by the king himself. Frederick's favorite visitors were French philosophes, many of whom received prestigious pensions and memberships in the Berlin Academy of Sciences and Belles Lettres.

Above all, there was Voltaire, whom the king fi-nally lured to Sanssouci in 1750 after years of mutu-ally adoring correspondence. But the famous king and the famous philosophe were both too vain to inhabit the same building for long. In 1753, Voltaire quarreled with a protégé of Frederick's and defied the king by publishing a savage satire. No longer wel-come at the Prussian court, the philosophe left for France; but halfway there he was overtaken, arrested, and briefly jailed by Frederick's agents, who confis-cated the medals and poems the king had given him. All Europe was titillated by the duel of egos.

However great his passion for witty and elegant conversation, Frederick was an enormously hard worker. He did not tamper with the administrative machine built by his father and the Great Elector, but he constantly traveled through his lands making surprise inspections. Indeed, he found it almost im-possible to delegate authority; after his death, the kingdom was ill prepared to carry on without him.

Though anecdotes abounded about Frederick's concern for his subjects and their loyalty to him, the king was anything but democratic. While he counted on the allegiance of noblemen, he tended to disregard peasants and townspeople except as a source of taxes. He reversed his father's practice of advancing worthy commoners; under Frederick the Prussian officers and higher bureaucrats were almost always aristocrats. Although the king encouraged agriculture, cottage industries, and an independent peasantry, he did so primarily to broaden the state's tax base. He did nothing to alleviate serfdom. In short, the Prussia of Frederick the Great was a rigidly stratified society, and the king did his best to strengthen, not weaken, the barriers between classes.

None-too-admiring contemporaries often said that Prussia was a large army with a small state attached. But in building the military—as in shaping society—Frederick merely followed his ancestors. His innovation was his daring use of his troops; as a strategist he took risks that would have appalled his father. His soldiers, like those of his father, were mercenaries not conscripts, who deserted without compunction and fought not for love of Prussia but for fear of the swagger sticks of their officers. The constant drill for which the Prussian army was famous was meant to ensure unbroken formations on the battlefield—an army of robots was ideal for the wars of maneuver typical of the eighteenth century.

Between 1756 and 1763, during the Seven Years' War, Prussia and its army were put to their severest test, and in this conflict Frederick the Great earned his reputation as one of Europe's greatest military leaders. In 1756 a "diplomatic revolution" astounded Europe, when through the success of Maria Theresa's superb diplomacy, Austria and France renounced their ancient enmity. The French Bourbons and the Austrian Hapsburgs were now allies, and the Russian czarina Elizabeth had joined them as well. Frederick thus found himself surrounded by enemies who began to refer to him as the marquis of Brandenburg, sug-

*bove, a detail from an allegorical painting
f Frederick the Great amidst celebration at
he end of the Seven Years' War.*

*Left, the battle of Kolín, which
signaled the end of Frederick's
Bohemian campaign. In this
battle, fought in June of 1757,
the French and Austrian troops
commanded by Frederick's per-
ennial rival—the Austrian
field marshal Count Leopold
von Daun—raised the Prussian
siege of Prague. Frederick was
defeated in this encounter.*

*Maria Theresa of Austria
(above) was Frederick's lifelong
enemy. She was also one of the
few women he admired. Below,
Maria Theresa's field marshal
Baron Gideon Ernst von Laudon at the battle of Kunersdorf
(now Kunowice, Poland) in
1759. At this battle, Frederick
suffered his most devastating
military defeat.*

gesting their intentions of cutting Prussia down to size. Only Britain supported Prussia—and as usual, with advice and subsidies rather than troops.

Although Frederick began the Seven Years' War with a pre-emptive strike into Saxony, his resources could not sustain a long offensive. For most of the war he fought on the defensive, and time after time he seemed on the verge of defeat. Even his brilliant generalship at such battles as Rossbach and Leuthen (Lutynia, Poland) in late 1757 and forced marches over astonishing distances to prevent hostile armies from uniting against him, could not have saved him without some exceedingly good luck. In 1759, after the catastrophic battle of Kunersdorf (Kunowice, Poland), Frederick's fortunes were at their lowest point. Russian troops occupied East Prussia and Berlin, and Frederick vowed, "I will not survive the destruction of my country." Yet, indifferent to his personal appearance or physical comfort, hardened and cynical, Frederick fought on, gradually winning the admiration of his troops.

In 1762 his luck suddenly changed. The czarina Elizabeth died, and her son, Czar Peter III, withdrew from the war. Exhausted, Austria and France also wanted to lay down arms, and in 1763 the Peace of Hubertusburg was signed. Prussia neither gained nor

Hapsburg Holy Roman emperor, Joseph II. B Frederick's real worry in the last years of his reign w Russia. To hold it at arm's length he signed a trea in 1764 with Czarina Catherine the Great, whic obliged him to help Russia make Poland a satellit Although Frederick had only contempt for obscuran Catholic, anarchic Poland, he feared that someday Polish revival might threaten Prussia. He therefo eagerly pressed the courts of Vienna and St. Peter burg to adopt a plan for Poland's partial dismembe ment. In 1772, Prussia, Austria, and Russia each a nexed a piece of Poland. Frederick's share was th smallest but most valuable segment—the land know as West Prussia, linking East Prussia with Pomeran and Brandenburg. Much later, in 1939, World Wa Two erupted over this territory, then known as th Polish Corridor.

Frederick the Great died in 1786, but his era die even earlier. Already French military tacticians we changing warfare by emphasizing broken-field ski mishing and artillery fire rather than the maneuve ing of infantry squares. The first winds of moder nationalism were blowing across the Continent an into Germany. Above all, the rigid, hierarchical vie of society and the state which Frederick had neve

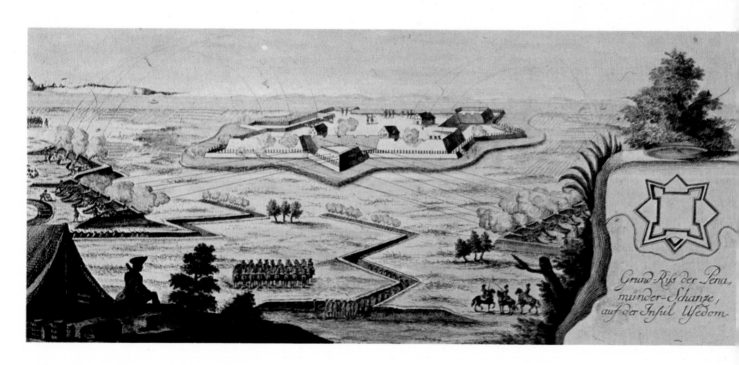

Grund-Rifs der Pena münder-Schantze, auf der Insul Usedom.

lost any territory. The agony of the war had served to maintain Prussia as a great power.

Between the end of the Seven Years' War and his death in 1786, Frederick worked to ensure Prussia's economic recovery and to maintain the balance of power in Europe, now relying mostly on diplomacy. He assumed the novel role of champion of the lesser German princes against the expansionism of the

questioned was losing support. The time of the En lightened Despots was gone. Old Fritz, as his subject called him with grudging affection, had left behind kingdom weary of his burdensome taxes and harass ing bureaucrats.

"Literature has never flourished on German soil, sneered Frederick not long before his death. The re mark is further evidence that the times had passe

In 1757 the Swedes besieged the Prussians at the fortress of Peenemünde (left), on Usedom Island, now part of East Germany. Above, General Friedrich von Seydlitz, a Prussian cavalry officer wounded at the battle of Rossbach in November of 1757. Below, plans for the battle of Leuthen (now Lutynia, Poland) at which Frederick the Great (right) defeated the Austrian army.

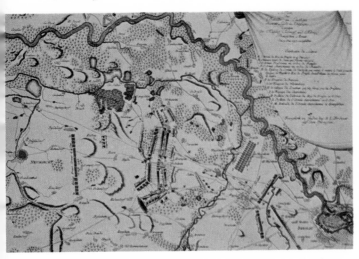

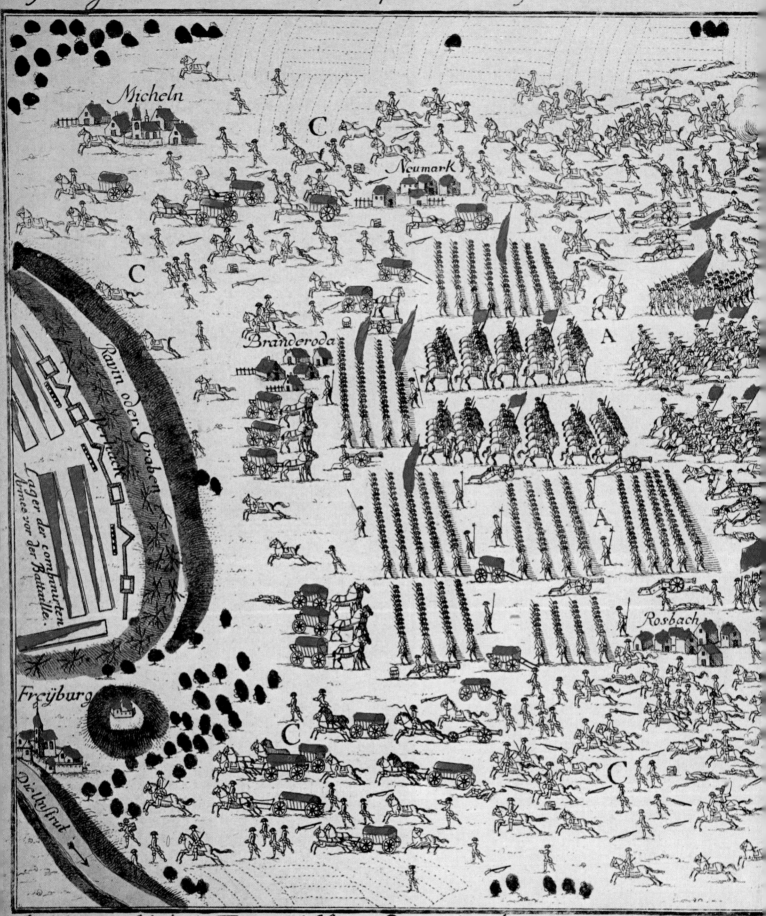

Micheln

C

Neumark

C

Branderoda

A

A

Ravin oder Graben

Lager der combinirten Armee vor der Bataille.

Freyburg

Die Unstrut

Rosbach

C

C

A. Die combinirte Französische und Reichs Armee. B. Die Preußische

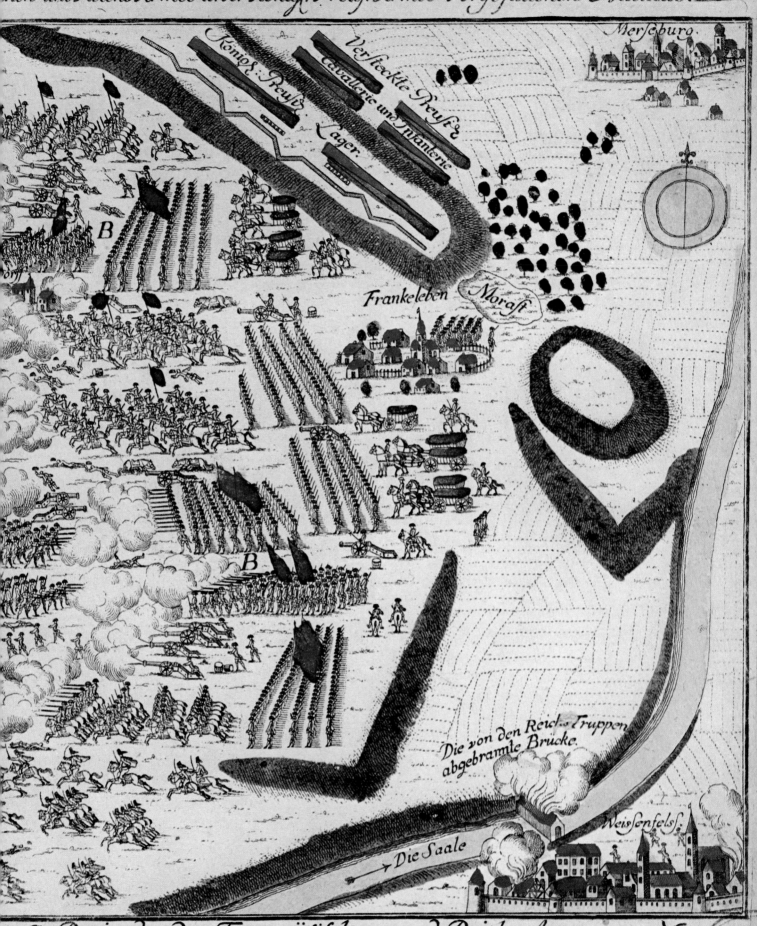

Merseburg.

Königl. Preuß. Lager.

Versteckte Preuß. Cavallerie und Infanterie

A

B

...orff

B

Frankeleben

Moraft

Die von den Reichs Truppen abgebrannte Brucke.

Die Saale

Weissenfelß.

him by, for in the 1780s German culture was entering its golden age. Johann Wolfgang von Goethe, one of a handful of giants in world literature, was well on the way to establishing his mature classicism. German Classicism preached the lofty doctrine that humanity could be nurtured by attention to the enduring realm of ideals. It respected human reason but found the rationalism of the French Enlightenment, so dear to Frederick the Great, cold and mechanistic. According to Goethe and his associates, humankind becomes more profoundly human by struggling through the formative and painful turmoil of life to the calm repose of spiritual wisdom. And the surest guide to that harbor is the human imagination.

Yet Prussia was not a center of German Classicism. The mecca of Classicism lay to the south, in Saxe-Weimar, where Goethe resided, acting as a court councilor to his friend Duke Karl August, and where he was later joined by the great dramatist Friedrich Schiller and others.

A second great movement in German letters did find a home in Berlin. The young leaders of early German Romanticism, August Wilhelm and Friedrich von Schlegel, Novalis, Tieck, and others, moved to the Prussian capital at the end of the century and published their seminal periodical, the *Athenäum*, there. These Romantics valued spontaneity and brooding introspection more than the decorous repose of Classicism. And all were profoundly influenced by the older Prussian-born thinker Johann Gottfried von Herder, who found the roots of the human experience in the natural spontaneity of the people. His research into folk history and culture set the stage for the wedding of German nationalism to German intellectual life.

While Herder and the Romantics were groping toward a sense of German nationhood and Goethe was displaying his usual Olympian detachment from nationalism and German politics, a philosopher in the East Prussian capital of Königsberg was training a whole generation of young men to think clearly about the German nation. Immanuel Kant never stirred from his little university town, where he taught nearly every subject in the curriculum, but he drew together most of the strands of the late eighteenth-century German cultural revival and of the earlier French and Scottish Enlightenment as well. After his writings on metaphysics, including such monuments as the *Critique of Pure Reason*, he turned his attention to the more down-to-earth questions of ethics, or "practical reason," beginning with the absolute duties of conscience. From there it was only a short step to questions of political morality.

Among Kant's students were many future army

Preceding pages, a schematic view of the battle of Rossbach, where 22,000 Prussians routed nearly twice as many French and Imperial troops. The élan of Seydlitz's cavalry contributed to the victory.

In October of 1758, Austrian troops under Daun surprised and defeated Frederick at Hochkirch (above), destroying nearly a quarter of his army. Daun and his colleague Laudon were worthy adversaries of Frederick during the Seven Years' War.

In 1760, Frederick the Great turned the tables by defeating Daun's troops at Torgau, on the Elbe River. Although wounded slightly (near left) and briefly unconscious, the king refused aid until victory was certain. He ended his day (far left) by recording orders while seated on the altar steps of the village church.

When the Prussian troops occupying Saxony were driven from Dresden in 1757, Frederick viewed the defeat of the Regiment of Anhalt-Bernburg as a disgrace. In 1760, though, the heavily outnumbered regiment fought so well at Leignitz that the king (above) restored it to full honor. Preceding pages, the famous siege of Olmütz (Olomouc, Czechoslovakia), an Austrian stronghold when Frederick invested it—unsuccessfully—in 1758.

These small round pictures (left), designed to be attached to gold and silver coins, depict Frederick as he customarily appeared to his subjects: in full uniform, preoccupied with his army, and often contemplative and withdrawn. He was seen as a war captain and philosopher, steadfast in both victory and defeat.

fficers and civil servants, who later led the reformation of the Prussian state. Such young men as Heinrich Friedrich Karl vom Stein, August von Gneisenau, and Gerhard von Scharnhorst were struck by Kant's idea that the state should justify its existence by being a school of civic virtue. For them, Kant, the German idealist, and Adam Smith, the Scottish economist whose ideas Kant helped to popularize, served as mentors in the effort to refashion Prussian economic and political life. Smith's insistence that all external restrictions on economic enterprise be swept away was in accord with the German idealists' appeal for the state to instill in its citizens a sense of moral self-regulation and public spiritedness.

Prussia under Frederick the Great presented an ambiguous image to the later German humanists: Its reputation as a bleak "garrison state," pursuing war and diplomacy as ends in themselves, was at odds with Frederick's view of himself as the "first servant of the state." Prussia was built on a rigid class structure, harsh military discipline, a heavy-handed bureaucracy, and a coldly calculating foreign policy—yet its king also championed religious toleration and the rule of reason. If the sense of political mission and discipline with which Frederick and his ancestors had ruled could be joined to the humanists' dream of a unified commonwealth of high purpose, then Prussia might indeed become the agent of Germany's regeneration. Such hopes led Stein, Gneisenau, Scharnhorst, and others like them into service of the Hohenzollerns as the century drew to a close.

In 1789, Europe was electrified by news of the fall of the Bastille, and then entranced as France began its painful transformation into a liberal constitutional monarchy. Many German humanists greeted the French Revolution with joy; from Königsberg, Kant acclaimed it as an unforgettable moment in human history. (To the astonishment of his neighbors, he even missed his regular afternoon stroll, when he was diverted by newspaper accounts of the fall of the Bastille.) The mob violence and fanaticism in Paris troubled the Germans, but even so, the spectacle of Europe's greatest nation shedding the shackles of autocracy and aristocratic privilege was compelling. Many hoped (while many others feared) that the death knell had sounded for absolute, caste-ridden monarchies such as the Prussia of Frederick the Great. Soon strident, reactionary voices deploring the Revolution's threat to social order and religion were heard from the lower nobility surrounding the thrones of German princes—who themselves were

nervous about France's invigorated military powe

In 1792 war broke out between France and th German states. Prussian troops under the duke Brunswick led an invasion of France, but suffered surprising defeat at Valmy in September. Goeth rightly descried a turning point in history: A citize army had beaten Frederick the Great's professional for all their precision tactics. War would never agai be the same.

After its defeat at Valmy, Prussia did not partic pate energetically in the war with Revolutionar France. Frederick's inexperienced and vacillatin nephew, Frederick William II, assumed the Prussia throne in 1786. His immediate preoccupation was th uneasy balance of power in eastern Europe. A reviv ing Poland caused concern, and in 1793 Frederic William joined Catherine the Great in seizing add tional chunks of Polish land. Two years later Polan exploded in a revolution led by the pro-French pa triot Thaddeus Kosciusko. Prussia, Austria, and Ru sia, alarmed by this outbreak of "Jacobinism," con spired to extinguish the Polish state altogethe Prussian rule was extended east to Warsaw.

In that same year, 1795, Frederick William II for mally withdrew Prussia from the continental war b signing the Treaty of Basel with republican France Prussia recognized French control of the entire lef bank of the Rhine, and the French Republic ac knowledged Hohenzollern hegemony over most c northern Germany. This separate peace brough Prussia a decade-long respite, during which time Na poleon Bonaparte rose to power and became emperor of France. Directly or indirectly, Napoleon rule many parts of western Germany, and there he intro duced the social and economic gains of the Frenc Revolution, to the special benefit of the middle clas The new French ruler imposed uniform law code

Popular prints (left) served to illustrat episodes in the life of the now legendary Fred rick the Great. From top: a soldier offers th exhausted monarch water carried in a tri corn hat; Frederick, alone and pensive, sit on a drum after his 1756 victory at Lobosit (now Lovosice, Czechoslovakia) assured th conquest of Saxony; the king watches sympa thetically as a general collapses in the arm of a soldier at the end of another battle of th Seven Years' War; a peasant woman show Frederick the hayloft near the battlefield o Torgau where she had earlier given birth

Voltaire

For nearly three years the French philosophe Voltaire lived at the palace of Frederick the Great, where he polished the king's French writing style and finished his own great *Century of Louis XIV*. The king and the philosophe both shared an admiration for elegant, sardonic rationalism and the witty sparkle of fashionable conversation, as well as a deep disdain for superstition and fanaticism. But their differences, too, were profound. Voltaire loathed war, while Frederick built his career on it. Although both were skeptics and anticlerical, Frederick protected the established Protestant Church for political reasons and even invited the Jesuits to Prussia, while Voltaire detested all organized religion and especially despised the Jesuits. Frederick had rather Spartan tastes; Voltaire loved his comfort and yearned for money and honors. These irreconcilable differences led to Voltaire's precipitous departure from Sanssouci.

A print (above) from an eighteenth-century series by Peter Haas shows Frederick the Great (left) and Voltaire as they stroll under the colonnade at Sanssouci Palace. They are accompanied by two of the king's constant companions—his prized Italian greyhounds, who often appear in paintings of Frederick. Voltaire's three-year sojourn at Sanssouci was a revealing testimony to the hazards of proximity: Conflict between Frederick and his distinguished guest were intense and frequent.

An engraving by P. C. Baquoy (left), after a sumptuous painting by N. A. Monsiau, depicts Frederick (standing) and Voltaire in the study at Sanssouci. As with most court paintings, the portrait idealizes their friendship; in reality, Voltaire was much too vain and cynical to pay court for long, and Frederick was too much of an absolutist to tolerate the criticism of his close companions. It was not a happy match.

Pandours

The first corps of pandours was recruited by the Austrian Hapsburg ruler Maria Theresa. Mostly of Croatian origin, these greedy, violent irregulars fought bravely for Austria during its first war with Frederick the Great. Not long after, Frederick's Prussia imitated Austria by establishing several pandour units of its own.

The pandours, who became a sort of eighteenth-century foreign legion, fought solely as light infantry in distinctive crimson Turkish-style uniforms. Because war booty was their only pay, they posed a terrifying threat to civilians as well as to traditional armies of the period, who were intimidated by their unpredictability.

Above, a Black Hussar in the army of Frederick the Great. These troops wore distinctive headgear called busbies, adorned with a skull and crossbones. Left, a Croatian soldier, and below, an irregular from the Croatian region of Morlacca, both in service to Austria.

Pandours were Croatian foot soldiers who served as irregulars in the Hapsburg armies before 1756 and as regular Austrian troops thereafter. The large picture (center) acknowledges the widespread reputation of the pandour as a wild, pillaging, undisciplined vandal. This word, which in Croatian simply signifies a "constable" or "guard," has in several Western European languages come to imply savagery or brutality. Nonetheless, pandour troops were valued by Maria Theresa; several of their uniforms are illustrated at far right. From top: a captain of the pandours; a pandour from Slavonia; and one of the pandour troops that performed peacetime frontier duty on the Hapsburgs' eastern borders.

and rational administrative methods and lifted restrictions on commerce and manufacturing. He decreed religious toleration and opened careers in government and the military to all, on the basis of merit rather than birth. But representative government was forbidden, and no sympathy was shown to budding German nationalism.

While "Herr von Bonaparte" was consolidating his regime in France and western Germany, Prussia acquired a new king. Frederick William III meant well; the French Revolution, he wrote, "provided a powerful, terrifying example to all bad rulers who, unlike good rulers, do not live for the welfare of their country, but like leeches suck it dry." Reformers such as Stein and Gneisenau gained the monarch's ear and urged a union of the Hohenzollern tradition of state service with the new civic humanism. They called on Prussians to serve their king as free men rather than as sullen serfs, terrorized soldiers, or arrogant officials. Some of the early Romantics, as they matured, supported the reformers in this patriotic appeal, and the writings of the poet Ernst Moritz Arndt and the philosopher Johann Gottlieb Fichte fired the young with Prussian and even German patriotism. But vested interests, especially among the Junkers, prevented a thorough overhaul of the state until after disaster

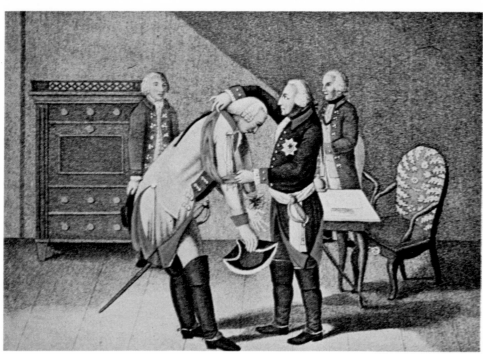

Frederick reviews the troops at Potsdam (preceding pages), decorates an officer (above), and in a satirical print (below), complains about having to "maintain" Czarina Elizabeth and Maria Theresa.

ruck, and Prussia met its greatest peril unprepared. "We went to sleep on the laurels of Frederick the Great," lamented Queen Louise.

In 1805, Frederick William III stood by while Napoleon defeated Austria at Austerlitz and abolished the Holy Roman Empire. A year later the king accepted the complacent assurances of his generals that the Prussian army could whip the French rabble unaided. So Frederick William went to war alone against Napoleon. Within days his army was crushed in the battles of Jena and Auerstedt. All over the country, garrisons surrendered without firing a shot. The bureaucracy collapsed. In a few weeks Napoleon

was in Berlin, then swept on to meet the Russians at Friedland in East Prussia.

The French conqueror came to terms with Czar Alexander I at Tilsit, a river town on the border between East Prussia and the Russian Empire. Prussia's fate was decided almost as an aside. The peace settlement left Prussia a third-rate power and a French satellite. Stripped of most of its Polish territorial acquisitions and of large land areas in north-central Germany, it retained only Brandenburg, Pomerania, East and West Prussia, and (as an inducement for good behavior) Silesia. Prussia was forced to pay heavy indemnities, to join Napoleon's embargo

As Frederick's legend grew, anecdotes about his life became the frequent subject of popular prints. Above center, Frederick forgiving a servant who confessed to a bungled attempt to taint the king's chocolate. The king's display of courage (near left) unnerves a potential assassin; when the assailant aimed at him from a bush in the royal park, Frederick simply stopped, pointed, and called reproachfully, "You, you!" The man did not fire. Above, an allegorical depiction of the Peace of Hubertusburg (1763), which ended the Seven Years' War between Prussia and the Franco-Austrian alliance.

Frederick the Great's royal residence at Sanssouci boasted a magnificent main building with a famous colonnade (right) as well as other remarkable structures, including the terraced greenhouses by the terrazzo park (below) and the separate Picture Gallery (above).

Sanssouci

During Frederick II's first war with Austria in 1740, he began making plans to build a tranquil retreat—the palace of Sanssouci. Designed by Georg Wenzeslaus von Knobelsdorff, this unusual royal residence is the most famous example of Prussian Rococo. Of a lighter, more delicate style than the Rococo of Bavaria or Austria, Sanssouci is modest in size, consisting of thirteen rooms, all located on one floor. Frederick, proud that he had not bankrupted Prussia with his projects, once commented, "I confess that I like to build and to decorate, but I do it with my own savings, and the State does not suffer."

Frederick's life at Sanssouci was quite simple, too, by royal standards. Only intimate friends, and a select group of accomplished musicians or conversationalists, were welcome. As the king aged, he invited fewer and fewer visitors. Frederick spent his later days at Sanssouci in relative isolation, surrounded by his work, a few servants, and his beloved greyhounds.

These photographs hint at the Rococo elegance of Sanssouci, and suggest its debt to Versailles. Top right, the Small Gallery in the east wing, decorated by Johann Christian Hoppenhaupt with paintings and busts of famous men. Immediately above, the Music Room where, surrounded by Antoine Pesne's paintings of scenes from Ovid's Metamorphoses, *Frederick held his nightly concerts. Right, the Vestibule, part of a succession of rooms forming the only passage to Frederick's study. Left, a view of the Great Park. Above left, the Entrance Gate, with the Corinthian colonnade of the Courtyard of Honor barely visible in the background.*

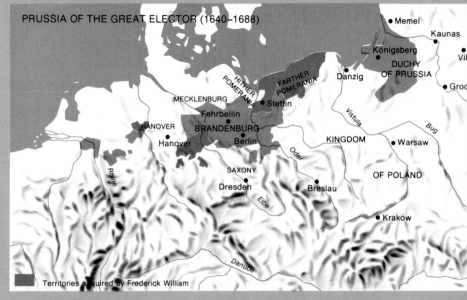

PRUSSIA OF THE GREAT ELECTOR (1640–1688)

Memel • Kaunas • Königsberg • DUCHY OF PRUSSIA • Danzig • Vil • Grod • HITHER POMERANIA • FARTHER POMERANIA • MECKLENBURG • Stettin • Fehrbellin • HANOVER • BRANDENBURG • Berlin • Hanover • Vistula • Bug • KINGDOM • Warsaw • Oder • SAXONY • OF POLAND • Dresden • Elbe • Breslau • Rhine • Kraków • Danube

Territories acquired by Frederick William

In 1640, Frederick William the Great Elector inherited the scattered Hohenzollern-ruled territories. His principal possessions were Brandenburg (an electorate of the Holy Roman Empire) and Prussia. These two domains became the nucleus of Prussia's future empire. Frederick William spent much of his reign trying to wrest Pomerania from the Swedes, seeking to provide Brandenburg with a seaport. Though he was victorious over Sweden, only part of Pomerania was under his rule at the time of his death in 1688.

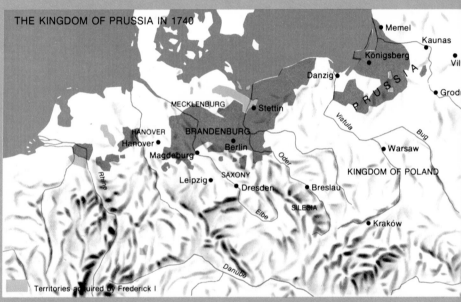

THE KINGDOM OF PRUSSIA IN 1740

Memel • Kaunas • Königsberg • Vil • Danzig • Grod • PRUSSIA • MECKLENBURG • Stettin • HANOVER • BRANDENBURG • Hanover • Magdeburg • Berlin • Vistula • Bug • Warsaw • Oder • KINGDOM OF POLAND • Leipzig • SAXONY • Rhine • Dresden • Breslau • Elbe • SILESIA • Kraków • Danube

Territories acquired by Frederick I

During the reign of the Great Elector's son Frederick, Prussia acquired part of Pomerania, including the valuable seaport of Stettin. In 1701, with the permission of the Holy Roman emperor, Frederick took the title "king in Prussia." The first Hohenzollern to claim this dignity, he extended royal leadership throughout his entire domain. Frederick William I, his son, contributed little to the territorial expansion of Prussia, but he built a peerless army that served as the basis for Prussia's future greatness.

PRUSSIA OF FREDERICK THE GREAT (1740–1786)

Memel • Kaunas • Königsberg • Vilr • Danzig • Grodn • EAST FRIESLAND • MECKLENBURG • POMERANIA • POMERELIA • PRUSSIA • Stettin • ✕ Kolín • HANOVER • BRANDENBURG • Münster • Hanover • Berlin • Posen • KINGDOM • Warsaw • KLEVE • Magdeburg • Kunersdorf • MARK • Leipzig • Torgau • Oder • OF POLAND • Cologne • SAXONY • Leuthen ✕ • ✕ Breslau • Rossbach • Dresden • SILESIA • ✕ Mollwitz • Elbe • Kraków • Olmütz • Rhine • Danube

Territories acquired by Frederick the Great

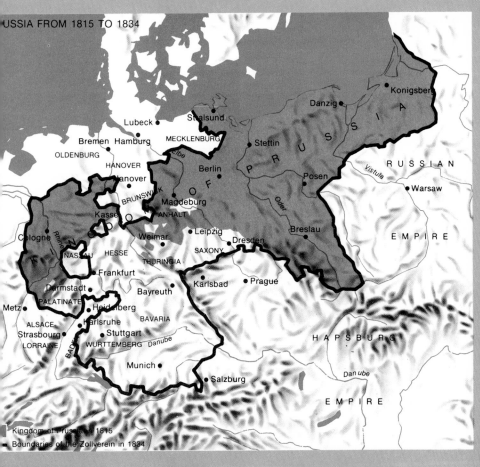

PRUSSIA FROM 1815 TO 1834

Königsberg
Danzig
Lubeck
Stralsund
MECKLENBURG
Bremen Hamburg
Stettin
OLDENBURG
Elbe
P R U S S I A
HANOVER
Berlin
RUSSIAN
Hanover
Posen
Oder
Vistula
BRUNSWICK
Warsaw
Magdeburg
EMPIRE
Kassel ANHALT
Cologne
Rhine
Weimar
Leipzig
NASSAU
Dresden
HESSE
Breslau
Frankfurt
THURINGIA
SAXONY
Darmstadt
Karlsbad
Prague
PALATINATE
Bayreuth
Metz
Heidelberg
ALSACE
Karlsruhe
BAVARIA
Strasbourg
Stuttgart
HAPSBURG
LORRAINE
BADEN
WÜRTTEMBERG
Danube
Munich
Dan ube
Salzburg
EMPIRE

▬ Kingdom of Prussia in 1815
▬ Boundaries of the Zollverein in 1834

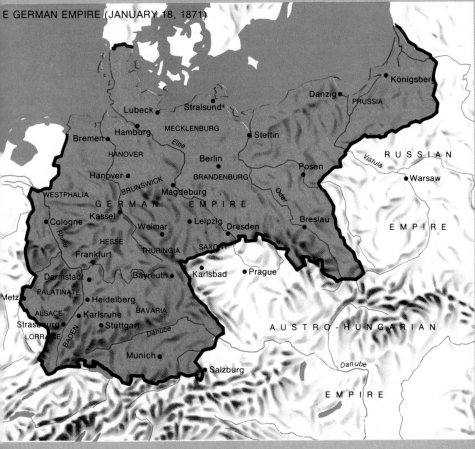

THE GERMAN EMPIRE (JANUARY 18, 1871)

Königsberg
Danzig
PRUSSIA
Lubeck
Stralsund
MECKLENBURG
Bremen
Hamburg
Stettin
HANOVER
Elbe
Berlin
RUSSIAN
Hanover
Posen
BRANDENBURG
Vistula
BRUNSWICK
Warsaw
WESTPHALIA
Magdeburg
G E R M A N   E M P I R E
Oder
Kassel
EMPIRE
Cologne
Weimar
Leipzig
Rhine
Dresden
Breslau
HESSE
Frankfurt
THURINGIA
SAXONY
Darmstadt
Bayreuth
Karlsbad
Prague
PALATINATE
Metz
Heidelberg
ALSACE
Karlsruhe
BAVARIA
Strasbourg
Stuttgart
BADEN
Danube
AUSTRO-HUNGARIAN
LORRAINE
Munich
Dan ube
Salzburg
EMPIRE

Frederick II the Great inherited the unmatched army of his father, Frederick William I, and used it to make Prussia one of Europe's major powers. In 1740, he forceably seized rich Silesia from the Hapsburg rulers of Austria. During the Seven Years' War, Frederick also attempted to annex Saxony, though with no success. His main additional territorial conquest came in 1772 when he diplomatically acquired Pomerelia from Poland. Now Prussian territory stretched to the Russian border.

The Congress of Vienna, which met in 1814–1815 to redraw the boundaries of Europe after the fall of Napoleon, greatly increased Prussian territory in western Germany and confirmed Prussian sovereignty over parts of Poland. The following years were marked by competition between Austria and Prussia for leadership over the German states. In 1834, with the establishment of the Zollverein (customs union), which deliberately excluded Austria, Prussia emerged as the dominant force in the burgeoning German economy.

In 1871 a Hohenzollern, King William I of Prussia, became emperor of the newly created German nation. The empire excluded only one major German-speaking group: the Austrians, whose Hapsburg rulers were the Hohenzollerns' main rival for control of the German state. However, many non-German nationalities lived within the empire's borders. This immense, polyglot German empire straddled middle Europe from Russia to Switzerland and from Holland to Hungary.

against British commerce, and—the greatest humiliation of all—to cut its once-renowned army to forty-two thousand men.

Defeat finally forced the reluctant Prussian monarchy onto the path of real reform. Frederick William III appointed Stein foreign minister, and later, in 1807, prime minister. Scharnhorst and Gneisenau also received prestigious positions. From 1811 on, another reforming minister, Prince Karl August von Hardenberg, led the cabinet. The new leaders conceded that Prussia had to remain Napoleon's satellite initially—at least until it could profit from a period of peace in which to rebuild. "Once in the Cyclops' cave, we can count only on the advantages of being devoured last," said Gneisenau, signaling Prussia's vulnerable position.

The reformers turned first to Prussia's shattered and shrunken army. In December of 1806 Frederick William III established a Military Reorganization Committee, headed by Scharnhorst and watched by suspicious old Junker officers who never trusted "foreigners" meddling with Frederick the Great's army. The reformers instilled a new spirit into a smaller army, recruited from a smaller territory. Soldiers in the ranks were now overwhelmingly Prussian-born. Townsmen as well as noblemen were eligible to compete, by examination, for commissions. Discipline was lightened, and there was less emphasis on drill and more on marksmanship. Soldiers learned the tactics of fighting in small, more mobile squads rather than massive lines and squares. The artillery was modernized, and in 1809 a civilian Ministry of War was established. The reformers clearly meant to build a citizen army modeled on that of France.

But if Prussian peasants and burghers were to fight successfully in a citizen army, they had to feel more genuine enthusiasm for king and country than they had shown in 1806. So the reformers moved to improve their lot. In October of 1807 the enserfed peasantry was emancipated. Practical economics as well as high ideals dictated this step: Because the 1806 war with Napoleon had ruined the land worked by the serfs, the state decided to free the peasants to shift for

Frederick the Great once boasted that he had received the royal city of Potsdam from his father "as a miserable hole and . . . left it a rich city." Although the remark was a little unfair to his forebearers, who had undertaken some impressive projects at Potsdam, it is true that Frederick was largely responsible for its splendor. One of his most impressive projects was the New Palace, which was built at the end of Sanssouci's park. Frederick commissioned its design from the French architect Jean Laurent Le Geay; its façade (below) and sumptuous Hall of Honor (left) display the enthusiasm for French taste that marked the king's entire reign.

Dresden

Dresden, the capital of Saxony, Prussia's rich neighbor to the south, was long an artistic center of Europe. By the eighteenth century, Dresden's famous Gallery of Paintings included works by Veronese, Tintoretto, Holbein, and Poussin. During these brilliant years, Baroque architects transformed the city into "the Athens of the North."

The ambition of the Saxon electors was evident not only in their sponsorship of the arts and their sumptuous and rather dissolute court life (rumor had it that Augustus III begot 350 bastard children), but also in their political entanglements. Yet, although they wangled election to the Polish throne, Saxon rulers never managed to play an independent role in eighteenth-century Europe. As for the Prussians, they associated Saxony with deceit and shameful opulence (Frederick William I dated his son Frederick's corruption from a visit the boy made in 1728 to the court at Dresden). At the same time, though, they viewed it as a tempting conquest. After becoming king, Frederick the Great invaded Saxony repeatedly and taxed it dry to finance his wars.

Frederick Augustus I (left), elector of Saxony, ruled Poland (1697–1733) as Augustus II, the Strong. An avid patron of the arts, he passed on the role to his son Augustus III of Poland (near right), who reigned from 1734 to 1763. The tradition of royal patronage transformed Dresden into one of Europe's most beautiful cities.

Left, a detail from a painting by Bernardo Belotto; the center figure is the artist himself. Belotto, an Italian painter related to the famed arti Antonio Canaletto, spent two long periods Dresden under the patronage of Augustus II While in Dresden, he painted two series of splen did oils of the city, including this view (righ across the Elbe River; the Hofkirche can be see under construction at right.

Another oil (left) from Belotto Dresden series shows the plaza the New Marketplace, and beyo it the ornate Baroque dome of t Frauenkirche. The building at l is the Stallhof (stables), the appa ent destination of the royal coa in the foreground. This painting from a series of fifteen large ca vases of Dresden that Belotto ex cuted in 1748–1749 for August III; the artist painted a simil series for Count Heinrich v Brühl, the influential prime mi ister of Saxony.

he Zwinger, one of Dresden's architectural ?ories, was a complex including an orangery and ?andstand, pavilions, galleries, gardens, and a ?rade ground for Augustus the Strong's beloved ?geants and tournaments. The king commis- ?ned his architect Matthäus Daniel Pöppelmann ? commence the project in 1711, yet it was still ?finished when construction was halted in 1722. ?bove, the Long Gallery, which displays an ornate ?le typical of the Zwinger. Right, a detail of a ?elotto painting depicting the moat of the ?winger as viewed from the Royal Orangery. Al- ?ough the complex was largely destroyed during ?orld War Two, the East German government ?s since partly restored it.

Berlin

Berlin, once a fishing village on the Spree River, had become the capital of Brandenburg by the late fifteenth century. In 1701, when the elector of Brandenburg crowned himself king in Prussia, he centralized the rule of all his domains in Berlin, which henceforth grew steadily in importance. By the nineteenth century, Berlin ranked as one of Europe's foremost cities.

Occupied by foreign armies in 1760 during the Seven Years' War, and again in 1806 under Napoleon, Berlin was spared extensive destruction until World War Two, when Allied bombing reduced much of it to rubble, and Soviet artillery nearly leveled the rest. Today only a few monuments of prewar Berlin endure, some of which have been restored—Charlottenburg, the Brandenburg Gate, a truncated Unter den Linden. The Berlin Cathedral remains in partial ruin, while the rubble of the Royal Palace has been cleared to make way for Marx and Lenin Square.

One of Berlin's most famous landmarks, the Brandenburg Gate (below) was built on the Pariserplatz at the end of the ceremonial boulevard Unter den Linden during the years 1788–1794. Johann Gottfried Schadow's famed sculpture of the Roman goddess Victory, riding in a chariot drawn by four horses, tops the Neoclassical colonnade designed by Carl Gotthard Langhans.

Above, an engraving of Berlin by George Balthasar Probst from the middle of the eighteenth century. At that time the city was surrounded by walled fortifications; it later grew to include many of its former suburbs. By the mid-nineteenth century, Berlin was known for its splendid wide boulevards, careful city planning, and impressive, if somewhat heavy-handed, public architecture.

Cityscapes of Berlin were popular in the nineteenth century. Above, the Brüderstrasse, with the Town Hall beyond the Fish Market, in the old quarter of Kölln; the cupola of the Petrikirche can be seen in the background. Near right, the plaza the Opera House looking toward the Royal Palace (which is not visible in painting). Far right, bottom, a partial view of the domed Berlin Cathedral (left), and the Royal Palace (center background), as seen from the Stock Exchange. Far right center, a view from Berlin's famed boulevard Unter den Linden toward the Royal Palace.

Above, the nephew and successor of Frederick the Great, Frederick William II (reigned 1786–1797). Near right, his son Frederick William III (reigned 1797–1840), who charted Prussia's unsteady course through the Napoleonic era. Well-meaning but irresolute, he initiated a series of reforms that eventually enabled Prussia to expel Napoleon from Germany. Far right, Frederick William III's wife, Queen Louise.

themselves. Similar motives led to the destruction of many central bureaucratic controls on urban economies. Barriers between the old social orders were removed, so that nobles or peasants could take up urban occupations and burghers could buy the land of their social inferiors or superiors. In 1811, Hardenberg abolished the guild regulations that restrained free enterprise.

Stein's efforts to reorganize the kingdom's upper administrative structure were only partly successful. He did arrange for each ministry to reflect a function rather than a territorial jurisdiction but he could not introduce the British principle of collective cabinet responsibility. The king preferred the traditional practice: Each minister reported individually to him, and until 1918 this procedure enforced royal influence over the administration. Stein also failed to convince Frederick William to call an advisory assembly representing all the Prussian estates, for the king was determined to avoid the fate that Louis XVI had unwittingly brought upon himself by summoning the French States-General in 1789.

One success of the reform era was the foundation of the University of Berlin in 1810 under the leadership of Goethe's friend Wilhelm von Humboldt, who later served as a political reformer as well. Humboldt in-

sisted on academic freedom at the university, and some of Germany's finest minds accepted chairs, including the philosophers Fichte and G. W. F. Hegel and the poet Heinrich von Kleist.

The reforms were planned and executed by the king and his ministers. The people did not help to shape policy, there was no representative government, and reforming ministers reported directly to the king. Although the prosperous middle class greeted the new freedoms joyfully, the peasants and artisans, who had enjoyed a measure of security behind "archaic" social barriers, were less eager to enter the bracing world of free economic competition. For much of the nineteenth century, Prussia and in fact all of Germany would struggle with the social problems raised by the reforms of Stein and Hardenberg.

While Prussia spent its energies on domestic reforms, Napoleon seemed as invincible as ever in Europe. Austria dared to challenge him once again in 1808, but Prussia and the rest of Germany would not follow its lead. King Frederick William III, morose since the death of his queen, Louise, in 1810, drove the patriotic reformers to despair by refusing to exploit the growing tensions between Russia and France and, worse still, by signing an alliance with Napoleon

in 1811. Subsequently, when the Grande Armée launched its ill-fated invasion of Russia in the spring of 1812, Prussian troops marched alongside.

Secretly, however, Frederick William had ordered Prussian troops to change sides if the Russian campaign went badly for Napoleon. As the remnants of the Grande Armée came staggering back through the snow in late 1812, Prussians began to remember that they were German, not French. On December 30, 1812, the Prussian commanding general declared his army neutral. Widespread discontent with French rule soon forced Frederick William into an open alliance with Russia, and in the appeal "To My Peo-

ple"—drafted by the reformers in March of 1813—h[e] called for a popular uprising against French domina[tion. By late summer the Austrian Empire also en[tered the fray, convinced that Napoleon could b[eaten at last. The War of Liberation had begun.

Now the success of the reformers' restructuring o[f] Prussian society became apparent. The middle classe[s,] at least were passionate in their support of the wa[r.] Arndt, Fichte, and other influential figures poure[d] out reams of patriotic writings. During 1813, som[e] three hundred thousand men—six percent of the pop[ulation—were called to the colors. The hard-drinkin[g,] colorful, astute old Junker general Gebhardt vo[n]

The Allied armies (near right), including the Prussian forces, muster for the battle of Leipzig. Napoleon's defeat here, in a three-day engagement fought by nearly five hundred thousand men during October 1813, led to his expulsion from Germany and ultimately to his exile on the island of Elba.

The Prussians pursued the fleeing French armies through the city of Leipzig (below). After the Allies succeeded in destroying a strategically located bridge, they captured many of Napoleon's troops; some 40,000 Frenchmen were taken prisoner and another 30,000 were killed or wounded at Leipzig's Battle of Nations.

lücher, at the head of the army, made Scharnhorst
nd Gneisenau his advisers. They proved a good
hoice. Scharnhorst died a hero's death, and Gnei-
enau, an excellent strategist, helped to shape the
lan that brought about Napoleon's defeat at the
attle of Nations near Leipzig in October of 1813.
Through victory, Germany was at last coming to
ealize that it was a nation. Writing to Hardenberg in
314, Gneisenau expressed the hopes of many edu-
ated and propertied Germans that Prussia would
ecome the moral leader of a regenerated Germany,
plendid in the three areas that alone enable a peo-
le to become great: military glory, a constitution

and the rule of law, and the flowering of the arts and
sciences."

Unfortunately, Prussia's neighbors and allies did
not share that dream. Austria and Britain were uneasy about Germany's new nationalistic fervor. Although Prussian troops were responsible for spear-
heading the Allied invasion of France in 1814 that led
to Napoleon's fall, and though they fought well at
Waterloo to prevent his return the next year, the
other Allies moved to curb Prussia's influence at the
peace talks in Vienna.

The Congress of Vienna, led by Austria's conservative, suspicious chancellor Klemens von Metternich,

After the fall of Napoleon, the mutually suspicious victors were confronted with the problem of preserving the balance of power, and in 1814 the Congress of Vienna met to redraw the boundaries of Europe. In this satirical print (right), Napoleon spies on the meeting from his island exile, while (left to right) Alexander I of Russia, Francis I of Austria, and Frederick William III of Prussia confer.

moved to clip Prussia's wings. The chancellor guided the creation of a German Confederation, which would permit Austria and a host of petty German states to hold Prussia in check. Prussia's aim at Vienna was to acquire Saxony and most of the remaining territories in central Germany, but its allies, except for Russia, conspired with defeated France against Prussian ambition. Prussia did not gain Saxony but instead received the territory of Poznań (Posen) in Poland, the coal-rich region of Saar on the French border, and considerable territories in the Rhineland.

In September of 1814, the final project of the Prussian reformers was approved by the king—universal military service. It is ironic that the draft, which to later generations seemed the essence of oppressive, militaristic "Prussianism," was at first considered dangerously radical, even "Jacobinical," by conservatives, who thought it almost subversive to arm the masses. Indeed, with demobilization, the new Prussian army was gradually shorn of its more "democratic" features, losing the draftees that had made it, to some extent, a citizens' army. The officer corps remained a bastion of the Junkers, and the professional officers began to feel distant from—and superior to—the civilian world. The citizenry and the mil-

itary regarded one another with deepening suspicion and the army became more than ever a closed and repressive caste.

By 1819, Prussia's period of liberal reform was over and it joined Austria and Russia as one of the champions of reactionary policy in post-Napoleonic Europe. The reformers had circumvented but not uprooted the entrenched conservatives in the government and among the Junkers. Yet nationalist and anticonservative sentiment was still strong in German universities, and in 1819 the Prussian government joined an Austrian-led crackdown on "subversive" activities among students. Hardenberg swam with the reactionary tide, but Humboldt and the other reformers in the Prussian cabinet were forced from office. Censorship and police repression returned. Constitutional government was out of the question.

Prussia's drift to the right in the 1820s coincided with the founding of the army's famous General Staff, whose function was parallel to that of the civilian Ministry of War in gathering intelligence and planning strategy. The hope of the reformers that the army would become a school of citizenship, encouraging loyalty among its members, was doomed, and

Left, the crown prince of Prussia, later Frederick William IV (reigned 1840–1861), on an equestrian outing in the company of the artist Franz Krüger. Impressed by the influences of Pietism and Romanticism, Frederick William revered the Middle Ages and combated the liberal ideology of the French Revolution.

Elsewhere in Germany, liberal ideas from France animated a vocal and well-organized opposition to absolutist government. This caricature (immediately below) is from the grand duchy of Baden; it pillories the conservative officials who imitated the antiliberal and militaristic attitudes of their Prussian counterparts.

Under Frederick William III and Frederick William IV, Prussia developed one of the most advanced systems of transportation in the world. Reliable postal carriages, such as the one at left dating from about 1826, carried passengers and baggage, as well as mail, along regularly scheduled routes. Below, a railway table reproduced from a contemporary women's weekly. The listings of trains departing from Berlin illustrate the complexity of the expanding rail network.

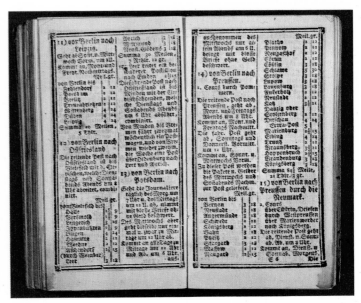

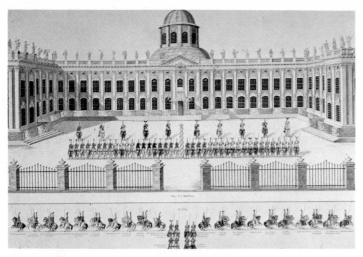

The pleasures of nineteenth-century royalty were lavish. To celebrate the birthday in 1829 of Alexandra, eldest daughter of Frederick William III and czarina of Russia by virtue of her marriage to Czar Nicholas I, the Prussian court organized the Festival of the White Rose (top left) at the New Palace in Potsdam. Each guest at the ball received a white rose from the czarina herself as a memento of the gala occasion. Immediately above, a "tableau vivant" at a Berlin ball. Left center, the great staircase of the Royal Palace of Berlin, in a mid-century painting by Carl Graeb.

Cafes (left), frequented by the emerging middle class, were conducive to open discussion of far-ranging popular subjects. In Prussia the conservative government dominated by the king and nobility effectively prevented the middle class from gaining political power, though the bourgeoisie was active in business and in culture.

The University of Berlin (below) was founded in 1810 by Wilhelm von Humboldt, who gave it an international reputation. The monument in the foreground was erected to honor Wilhelm's brother Alexander von Humboldt, the Berlin scientist and traveler.

the best Prussian military thinkers of the period began to sound an ominously illiberal note. In his brilliant book *On War,* General Karl von Clausewitz declared that "war is the continuation of policy by other means." Future conflicts, he wrote, would pit entire armed peoples against each other, and the eighteenth century's battles of maneuver and negotiated settlements would give way to wars fought to annihilate enemy forces swiftly and totally. Under these circumstances, he concluded, the army must remain independent of civilian control. The state must mold its citizens' character, and not the reverse.

Clausewitz thus abandoned the noble ideal of the citizen army to develop the military as an instrument of state policy; his ideas found parallels in the conservative theories of other, even greater Prussian thinkers. The noted historian Leopold von Ranke, of the University of Berlin, saw the state as the driving force of history. All else, including social and economic life, was secondary to the concerns of the state—war, diplomacy, and political intrigue. The famous Berlin philosopher Hegel likewise glorified the state as the highest form of rational social organization. He advanced the revolutionary ideas that change is more fundamental than stability and that whatever is real is rational; he could therefore accommodate himself with equal ease to the French Revolution and to the reaction in postrevolutionary Prussia. By the 1820s he was hailing the Prussian state as the supreme incarnation of reason.

For the Prussian middle class after 1815, such political philosophies scarcely interrupted the tranquillity and coziness of life. It was the Biedermeier period, a time of consoling domestic *Gemütlichkeit* (warmth), of comfortable furniture and dreamily romantic culture. German music was in its glory, although Prussia was not a great musical center like the Vienna of Beethoven and Schubert or the Saxony of Weber, Mendelssohn, Schumann, and the young Wagner. But Berlin was a center of architecture; the splendid classical revival structures of Schinkel set the standard for public buildings throughout central Europe.

Beneath the stately, quiet surface, though, tremendous social change was underway. Between the end of the Napoleonic Wars in 1815 and the revolutionary year of 1848, the kingdom's population increased by almost forty percent. With the abolition of guild controls and with the aid of other liberal legislation of the French and reform-era Prussian governments, industrial capitalism boomed, especially in textiles, coal mining, and metallurgy. First the Rhineland and later Saxony and Silesia became manufacturing centers, as the Industrial Revolution spread. Across Prussia and the rest of Germany, joint-stock compa-

1848

News of the revolutions of February 1848, which drove conservative governments from power in Paris and Vienna, astonished—and then galvanized—the middle-class citizens of Berlin. In March the Berliners began to rise up against the absolute powers of their own king, Frederick William IV. Suddenly and dramatically, royal authority collapsed, and by April the king had withdrawn the royal troops from Berlin, accepting the protection of a citizens' Civic Guard. He charged an assembly with writing a constitution, curtailed censorship, and allowed freedom of assembly.

Over the summer, however, bickering increased between middle-class revolutionaries, jealous for property rights, and the more radical working classes. By November the king had recovered enough nerve to act on his true conservative prin-

ciples, sending royal troops back into Berlin to disarm its citizenry. He then dismissed the Constituent Assembly and imposed a constitution of his own, which left control of the army and the government in his hands. The reign of liberalism had had its day—now it was the turn of Bismarck's "blood and iron."

The muddled intransigence of Frederick William IV (above left) led to a short-lived victory by the liberal middle class. During the night of March 18, 1848, citizens erected barricades throughout Berlin. Above, the barricade in the Breitenstrasse. Below, the Alexanderplatz.

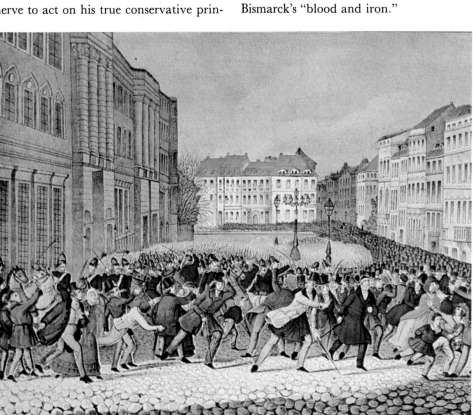

The Berlin revolution began on March 18, 1848, when the king's cavalry fired on an unarmed crowd near the Royal Palace (above). By late summer, when street mobs attacked the house of the royal official Rudolf von Auerswald (left), the king's troops had long been withdrawn from the city.

*ter the victory of the liberals at the Alexander-
atz barricade (top right), more radical elements,
me calling for an end to private property, began
ging their views. In August a demonstration in
harlottenburg (second from top, right) was bru-
lly suppressed.*

*Elaborate funerals (right) were
held on March 22, 1848, for the
"martyrs for liberty," who had
been killed by royal troops. Even
the king, who had been forced to
withdraw his troops, stood bare-
headed with his family as the dead
were paraded before him in the
palace courtyard. But after the
declaration of a state of siege
(above) in November, the middle-
class Civic Guard was disarmed by
the royal forces.*

Shortly after Frederick William IV went mad in 1857, his brother (left) became King William I. In 1871, Otto von Bismarck (above) had him named emperor of Germany.

nies, steam-powered riverboats, and railroads made men's fortunes. In 1834, Prussia formed a customs union, the Zollverein, with some smaller German states. The union sought to encourage commerce by removing customs restrictions on trade among the union's members and by creating a consistent policy of taxation on trade with nonmember countries. The Zollverein's potential as a nucleus for the political unity and aggrandizement of Germany was not lost on contemporary observers.

But the social costs of economic modernization were extremely high. Business crises occurred regularly every decade, bringing waves of bankruptcy.

Liberal legislation, which freed the serfs and destroyed the guild privileges of artisans, also turned them loose in a brutal market, and few could withstand hard times and capitalist competition. East of the Elbe River, Junker landlords, who were suffering from chronic collapses of the grain export market, expropriated the holdings of their former serfs and made hired hands of entire villages.

In Prussia's western provinces a growing rural population left the farms for the cities. Berlin's population soared to 400,000 in 1848—but only 20,000 held enough property to be taxed. Living conditions and factory pay were dismal. Child labor reached such

ppalling dimensions that the government had to
npose regulations lest the pool of physically fit mili-
ry recruits dry up. Even so, factory workers were
ell-off compared to the more numerous artisans,
ho could not hope to compete with the new indus-
ialized labor force. Organizing, agitating, emigrat-
g to America, occasionally rioting and smashing
achinery, Prussia's artisans fought a losing battle
gainst inflation, rising taxes, and industrial capital-
m. In 1844, Silesia exploded in an uprising of starv-
g small-town linen weavers, who were sup-
ressed only by the army's bloody reprisals. Industrial
roduction could not keep pace with the population,

Bismarck's first great military triumph was the lightning-fast war he incited against Austria in 1866. The immediate result of this Seven Weeks' War was the annexation of Hanover (far left, below), Hesse-Darmstadt, Hesse-Nassau, and three Danish duchies into Prussia's North German Confederation. The war's long-range effect was to exclude a weakened Austria from playing any role in a unified Germany. When the Prussians founded the German Reich, or Empire, in 1871, Austria was not even a part of it. Above, episodes from the Austro-Prussian War, as depicted in a Prussian children's game.

The first important battle of the 1866 war resulted in a Prussian victory over the Hanoverians at Langensalza (left). The decisive conflict, however, occurred in Moravia, near many of Frederick the Great's famous battlefields. There, at Königgrätz, Prussian armies led by such generals as Count Helmuth von Moltke (accompanied by William I and Bismarck, below) and Count Gottlieb von Haeseler (right) crushed the Austrians.

and by 1848 it was estimated that a tenth of Berlin's people managed to live only by prostitution and crime.

No one held out much hope to the poor in early nineteenth-century Prussia. Liberalism and nationalism were creeds of the well-fed middle class, who profited from industrial expansion, bought up the estates of bankrupt nobles, and longed for a constitution that would unify Germany while it guaranteed property rights and free enterprise against the mobs below and the bureaucrats above. Such concerns meant nothing to peasants, artisans, and factory workers; many still clung to the hope that their fatherly king, Frederick

William III, would learn of their troubles and sav them. By the mid-1840s, it is true, Karl Marx and h friend Friedrich Engels were starting to preach prol tarian revolution, but they had only scorn for bacl ward-looking artisans and for "rural idiocy." Th Prussians most attentive to the plight of the workin classes were political reactionaries—especially the ac visers surrounding Frederick William IV, the wel meaning but temporizing new king who ascended th Prussian throne in 1840.

Frederick William's friends traced Prussia's misfo tunes back to Stein and Hardenberg. They advise the king to win back the loyalty of the masses b

After the victory at Königgrätz, William I decorated his son Crown Prince Frederick with the coveted Order of Merit (left). The prince, who later became Emperor Frederick III of Germany, had distinguished himself while commanding one of Prussia's two armies. His rather liberal ideas, however, had at first led him to oppose Bismarck's warmongering policies.

In 1866 the south German state of Bavaria allied itself with Prussia against Austria. The Bavarian army (below), in review for its king, Ludwig II, also helped Prussia defeat the French during the Franco-Prussian War.

estoring guild regulations, thereby retarding capital-sm. As a young man Frederick William had been namored of the Romantic movement and he shared s veneration of the Middle Ages. He favored the lea of returning the economy and the state to their recapitalist, prerevolutionary condition. But although he dreamed of becoming a universally beved autocrat, he was a talker not a doer. Only when severe depression in 1847 led to famine and mounting unrest was he jolted into action. The king convoked an advisory United Diet, and the middle-class epresentatives immediately raised the question of a onstitution. "Never will I permit a written sheet of paper to come between our God in heaven and this land . . . to rule us with its paragraphs and supplant the old sacred loyalty," vowed the king. The Diet broke up in mutual acrimony, and violent hunger riots exploded in the streets of Berlin.

In March of 1848, revolution engulfed all of Germany, touched off by news that revolutions had ousted King Louis Philippe in France and Metternich in Vienna. In Berlin, mobs once again took to the streets. Nervous troops, alienated from civilian life, fired on the demonstrators, and nearly leaderless citizens erected barricades for a night of bloody street fighting. Frederick William IV panicked and moved to conciliate the liberals he had scorned less than a year before. He ordered his troops out of Berlin, then rode through the streets wearing the red, black, and gold cockade of the German nationalists. He paid tribute to the rioters shot down by his own army and promised a constitution. By the end of March a liberal ministry had been formed, elections for a Prussian National Assembly had been announced, and the capital was garrisoned by a middle-class Civic Guard.

Throughout Germany, liberals and nationalists rejoiced that the moment to unite the fatherland had finally arrived. Liberal ministries were hastily installed everywhere, and at Frankfurt the Diet of the Confederation gave way to an elected parliament charged with writing Germany's new constitution. When the Prussian National Assembly met in Berlin, it too began to pave the way for Prussia's entry into the new united Germany.

But this "springtime of the peoples" quickly turned to winter. The first fissure appeared between the middle-class liberals and the working classes. Peasants and artisans scorned the parliaments; instead they preferred violent demonstrations against residual feudal dues and industrial capitalism, and showed scant respect for the property rights so dear to the liberals. In return, the middle class viewed th artisans and peasants as a mob unworthy of the vo for parliamentary representation. As Marx correct discerned in reviewing the complicated events 1848, the interests of bourgeois and proletarians we too divergent for them to make common cau against the reactionaries.

Another split appeared between German and Sl vic nationalists. The Slavic populations of Bohem and of Prussia's Polish provinces shocked Germa liberals by showing no enthusiasm for being swa lowed up into Greater Germany, no matter how li eral its constitution. So the groups that were fir united by their grievances against the government Prussia's conservative monarchy turned on each oth instead, and the reactionary forces, still intact, move in for the kill.

The conservatives, who still controlled the Prussia army, surrounded the king at Sanssouci, where h had retreated from the wrath of his liberal subjects i Berlin. Shrewd reactionaries, such as the Junker Ott von Bismarck, conciliated their peasants and waite for the revolutionary camp to splinter. In October 1848 the bourgeois Civic Guard shot down demor strating workers in Berlin. Liberals had begun fo lowing the reactionaries' own slogan: "Against dem

On August 16, 1870, General von Moltke informed King William I (left) of the Prussian victory at Rezonville, near the city of Metz in northeastern France. French marines (immediately below) heroically oppose the Bavarians, Prussia's allies, at Bazeilles. The French commander MacMahon tried to send his troops to aid Bazeilles, but he was surrounded and defeated at Sedan on September 1. The French debacle there led to the fall of Napoleon III, and on September 18 the Prussians besieged Paris. Bottom, a photograph of Moltke and his general staff directing the siege of the French capital.

1870 the nervous French government ...ked for a guarantee of Prussia's peaceful ...entions from William I, who was then ...king a cure at the south German resort of ...ns. Although the king reassured the ...ench, Bismarck used the king's report to ... Berlin government to provoke France, ...king public an altered, inflammatory ver-...n of the "Ems telegram." A few days later, ... July 19, France declared war on Prussia. ... the king's return to Berlin, Bismarck met ...n at the station (left) with the news.

The siege of Paris

During the reign of Frederick the Great and again during the Napoleonic era, Prussia was embroiled in wars against France. But the Franco-Prussian War of 1870–1871 sowed the most bitter harvest of hate between the two nations. The sudden collapse of Napoleon III's armies and government, and the defeatism of the Third Republic, were a source of shame for generations of Frenchmen.

Nonetheless, the people of France, as distinguished from its leaders, fought heroically against the Prussian invasion. Even after the surrender of the principal French armies at Sedan and Metz in the fall of 1870, Paris withstood an epic siege for four months. Its defenders, unable to link up with French forces in the provinces despite desperately fought sorties, finally succumbed to the Prussian strangulation of their food supplies. Yet even starvation could not subdue the city fast enough to satisfy Bismarck. The Prussian chancellor,

fearing the intervention of England and Russia, eventually persuaded King William I to authorize the bombardment of the city. Heedless of civilian casualties, the Prussians opened fire with five hundred Krupp cannons, and the French were forced into submission. The war cost France 140,000 lives, the loss of Alsace and Lorraine, and indemnities of five billion francs. The legacy of Franco-German mistrust has lasted through the two world wars to the present.

Blumenthal. Kronprinz v. Preussen

The outer ramparts of Paris at Bourget, defended by the troops General Budritzki (left), fell last to Prussia on October 1870. The desperate French tempt in December to regain th led to the bloodiest fighting of siege.

The French general Comte Maurice de MacMahon (left) was defeated and captured by the Prussians at Sedan. Set free after the war, he led a bloody assault on defiant Parisian radicals, crushing their newly established Paris Commune, and placing the city under the control of the Provisional Government at Versailles. Later, as president of the Third Republic, he worked unsuccessfully for the restoration of the French monarchy. Below, a map showing the defenses of Paris against the Prussian siege.

low, William I, Moltke, and smarck (center, left to right) ring the bombardment of Paris. e enormous cannons were made Krupp, the munitions firm ose name became synonymous th the German military industal complex.

Above, a lithograph of William I (center) surrounded by his celebrated Prussian generals during the Franco-Prussian War. Below, Parisian defenses viewed from within. The French mobilized every ablebodied male to defend their capital. The French leader Léon Gambetta made a spectacular escape from the surrounded city in a balloon to raise more troops in the provinces. But enthusiasm alone could not hold off the Prussians, who were better organized and more numerous. A starving Paris fell on January 28, 1871.

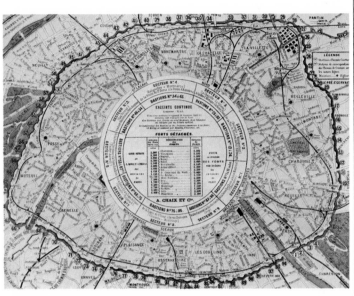

Prussia's victories cost France dearly. In September 1870, Napoleon III (above, in a carriage escorted by Bismarck on horseback) was captured at Sedan and forced to abdicate and seek exile. The Third Republic, which replaced him, could scarcely offer resistance. On March 1, 1871, recently triumphant Prussians paraded down the Champs-Élysées (above, near right), where some of them remained encamped (below, near right). Immediately below, Crown Prince Frederick of Prussia decorating some of his victorious troops with the new Prussian medal, the Iron Cross, at Versailles.

crats, only soldiers can help." In November, Frederick William recovered his nerve and sent regular troops back into Berlin. There was no resistance. A reactionary ministry was formed and the National Assembly sent home. The king immediately promulgated an authoritarian constitution that contained a few liberal phrases but maintained the substance of royal power, including control of the army.

The all-German liberal parliament in Frankfurt initially fared better than the Prussian revolutionaries. In March of 1849 it finally proposed a constitution for a federal German Empire, and a delegation traveled from Frankfurt to ask Frederick William to

become the constitutional emperor of a liberal Germany. He declined the offer, declaring in a private letter that he would not be "a serf of the revolution of 1848." The spurned liberals went home.

The Prussian king did intend to lead a united Germany, though. He merely hoped that the other German princes would join him to impose a more conservative union. With that hope in mind he sent troops in May of 1849 to Saxony and southwestern Germany to suppress demonstrations by radical democrats there. But Frederick William reckoned without Austria, which did not intend to let Prussia dominate Germany without a challenge. In early 1850, Vienna

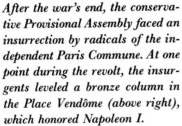

After the war's end, the conservative Provisional Assembly faced an insurrection by radicals of the independent Paris Commune. At one point during the revolt, the insurgents leveled a bronze column in the Place Vendôme (above right), which honored Napoleon I.

The French government suppressed the members of the Commune with merciless force. MacMahon's soldiers used artillery against their own countrymen while Prussian occupation troops stood by; the desperately resisting Communards burned the Tuileries (right). By the end of May 1871, the government was in control, but over 20,000 Parisians were dead and 38,000 arrested.

forced Prussia to sign the Olmütz Punctation, which restored the authority of the conservative princely states in Germany.

Although the revolutions of 1848 failed in Germany, throughout Europe they upset the social and international organization husbanded so carefully since the Congress of Vienna. Modern nationalism had come to stay, and the effects of industrial capitalism were irreversible, even if reactionary governments had finally learned to turn national and social grievances to their own profit.

Frederick William IV, who went mad in 1857, left his authority and finally his crown to his brother William I. By 1861, William recognized that the conservative reaction against capitalism had failed. He was now ready to ally himself with the middle-class industrialists, but insisted on retaining control of the army and the bureaucracy. The prospects of the bourgeoisie revived with the return of a bullish economy in the 1850s; the emigration of over one hundred thousand artisans and peasants, mostly to the United States, aided the boom. As capitalism resumed its advance, so did nationalism. Prussia and Austria again began vying for leadership of a united Germany capable of confronting a newly prosperous French Empire.

The stage was set for the last act in the drama of Prussia's rise to empire, and for its star, Otto von Bismarck. The ultrareactionary of 1848 had spent the next ten years as a Prussian diplomat in Frankfurt, Paris, and St. Petersburg. Although his contempt for liberalism had deepened, and his first and last loyalties were to the Prussian monarchy and to the Junkers, he had the intelligence to realize that the old political order could survive only by adapting to modern capitalism and nationalism.

In 1862, William I was locked in a struggle with the liberal majority in the Prussian Diet over control of army appropriations. He made Bismarck prime minister, and the blunt, crafty Junker broke the deadlock by simply defying constitutional niceties. The king's government collected taxes and re-equipped the army without parliamentary approval—and then forestalled liberal objections by using the military in an aggressive nationalistic foreign policy. In 1864 Bismarck sucked Austria into a war to "recover" the German-speaking provinces of Schleswig and Holstein from the Danish crown. Then in 1866 he picked a quarrel with Austria over the administration of these conquered provinces, and chose the same moment to propose a radical revision of the German Confederation, attempting to place Prussia in a more influential role in German affairs. Most German states, apprehensive about Prussia's new aggressiveness, elected to side with Austria in the ensuing Seven Weeks' War.

The splendidly reorganized Prussian army quickly defeated neighboring Hanover and then crushed the Austrians at the stunning battle of Königgrätz, in Moravia. The shrewd Bismarck foresaw that Austria would make a useful ally in the future, so he treated it generously at the peace table, only ensuring its exclusion from German affairs. After the annexation of Hanover and some other small northern German states and the establishment of the new North German Confederation, Prussian territory stretched unbroken from the Dutch to the Russian borders. "Germany does not look to Prussia's liberalism," Bismarck vaunted, "but to her power—Prussia must keep her power together for the auspicious moment, which already has been missed a few times. . . . The great questions of the day are not settled by speeches and majority votes—this was the error of 1848–1849—but by blood and iron." The liberal nationalists and capitalists applauded, and forgave his violations of the Prussian constitution.

"Blood and iron" soon won their culminating victory. Bismarck provoked France into declaring war on Prussia in 1870. Allied with the rest of Germany, Prussia crushed the French Empire's ill-prepared army at Sedan, then settled into a frightful siege of Paris. In January of 1871, as huge Prussian guns bombarded the beleaguered French capital, and as starving Parisians killed the zoo animals and hunted rats, William I was proclaimed German emperor before the assembled German princes and Prussian generals in the Hall of Mirrors at Versailles. Prussia had led Germany to unity on Prussian terms. It had reached a destiny that would have astonished even Frederick the Great.

Right, a German print commemorating the Franco-Prussian War and other events leading to the unification of the Reich. The first German emperor, William I (reigned 1871–1888, top center) is shown with his son (left), who succeeded him as Emperor Frederick III for ninety-nine days before he died of throat cancer, and with William II (reigned 1888–1918), Frederick's son, who led Germany into World War One. The Iron Cross (center), instituted during the Franco-Prussian War, is flanked by the two architects of that victory, Bismarck (left) and Moltke. Bottom center left, the proclamation of the Reich.

Hoch
lebe, wer mit Ehren
Gewehr u Waffen tragt,
Wem treu für Reich u Kaiser
Ein Herz im Busen schlägt,
Hoch
leben die Soldaten,
Zu Fuß u hoch zu Roß,
Im Kriege wie im Frieden
Vor Feind in Burg
und Schloß

Prussia's amazing rise in the seventeenth and eighteenth centuries to the status of a great power and its success in imposing unity on nineteenth-century Germany are sometimes presented as the victory of force—of "blood and iron"—over innocence. In 1947, for example, the victorious Allies of World War Two formally abolished Prussia as a political unit, charging that it had "from earliest days . . . been a bearer of militarism and reaction in Germany." But Frederick William the Great Elector, Frederick the Great, and Bismarck were men of high ideals; they sought their country's good. It is true that they built Prussia on the foundation of the monarchy and the army, for they considered that their success vindicated militarism and absolutism. What they failed to recognize was that rightful ends can become corrupt when evil means are used to reach them. Is it fair to blame these men for the use to which Emperor William II and Adolf Hitler put German militarism and absolutism during the world wars? Perhaps not. Perhaps the blame belongs with a wider circle—with those of the nineteenth and twentieth century who allowed the old ideals to become smug clichés, while the army came to embody patriotism, while patriotism itself became a reactionary force, and while the notion of popular sovereignty and the tradition of civil liberties suffered a mortal blow.

Napoleon and Europe

ean Jacques Rousseau, in his 1762 essay *The Social Contract*, warned that establishing a state based on popular sovereignty would not be easy. Above all, he wrote, the young democracy must be fortunate enough to escape the twin calamities of war and economic collapse if it is not to become easy prey for a dictator. "Usurpers always bring about or select troublous times," Rousseau contended. "The moment chosen is one of the surest means of distinguishing the work of the legislator from that of the tyrant."

The author of these lines would have had little trouble understanding the events that led to the cre-

Versailles (above) was the favored royal res dence of the later Bourbon kings of Franc and a symbol of their absolute power. Und Louis XVI (reigned 1774-1792), its popula tion of courtiers, royal functionaries, an servants exceeded sixty thousand and i budget consumed one fourth of the nonmil tary expenditures of the French state. Befor the French Revolution, the French system o government revolved around the king. Lou XVI (far left) was a weak and indecisiv ruler. His queen, Marie Antoinette (nea left), was an Austrian princess whose extra vagant ways added to antimonarchist feeling

ation of the First French Empire. He would never have imagined, however, that the founder of this empire would be from Corsica—the European nation singled out in *The Social Contract* as having a unique potential for developing a democratic constitution.

In 1765, when the Scottish writer James Boswell visited Corsica at Rousseau's suggestion, his imagination, too, was stirred by the rugged islanders, who were celebrating the end of a long struggle against Genoese domination. Quick to violence, devoted to family and clan, fond of oral poetry and song, the Corsicans were ready-made romantic heroes. Moreover, the island's deep-rooted poverty had prevented the growth of the great fortunes and entrenched privileges that were widely recognized as barriers to progress in the more developed European nations. In the flush of his enthusiasm, Boswell portrayed the Corsi-

cans as Europe's noble savages. "The men are goo fighters, but poor workers," he wrote. "They love, lik the American Indians, to lie around a fire and talk.

The reality of the Corsican situation was far dif ferent from the picture painted by Boswell. Pasqual di Paoli, who had commanded Corsican force against the Genoese, faced a formidable task i maintaining a sense of unity in a country where ther were few roads and fewer schools and where the tra dition of family vendettas undermined respect fo civil law. Unimpeded, Paoli's government migh have in time fulfilled the promise that Rousseau an Boswell saw in it; however, renewed foreign interven tion was soon to strip the island of its recently gaine independence.

Realizing that it would never be able to reassert it authority, the Republic of Genoa bartered its clain

the island to the French, and in August 1768—only few months after Boswell published the account of is travels—a French expeditionary force landed at e Corsican capital of Ajaccio. Paoli's supporters fled the mountains, where they launched a spirited uerrilla resistance, but the professionally trained and ell-equipped French soldiers were not as easily dis-dged as the Genoese had been. By March 1769 the rench were in control and Paoli had been driven to exile.

Three months after the French takeover, nineteen-ear-old Letizia Buonaparte, who had followed her usband, Carlo, to the partisan strongholds of the ountains, was back in the family home at Ajaccio. n August 15 she gave birth to her second surviving ild, Napoleone—the first member of the family to egin life as a French citizen.

Both Napoleone and his older brother, Joseph, grew up speaking Corsican-accented Italian. But in 1778, when Joseph and Napoleone were ten and nine years old, Carlo took them to France and enrolled them in the *collège* (secondary school) at Autun, where they could begin to familiarize themselves with the French language. This was only the beginning of Carlo's plans for his sons, and within a few months he had managed to secure a scholarship for one of them at the military preparatory school in Brienne. Carlo

apparently had no difficulty in deciding which of h[is] two sons had the makings of a soldier. Joseph r[e]mained at Autun to commence his preparation for [a] career in the Church, while Napoleone moved on [to] the strict regimen of Brienne.

One can easily imagine the difficulties faced by th[e] young Corsican, small in stature, unsure of the la[n]guage, and frequently forced to defend the reputati[on] of a homeland so recently humiliated by the army f[or] which he was being trained. Napoleon (he droppe[d] the final "e" from his first name soon after coming [to] France) was good at mathematics, poor at writi[ng] and spelling, and very poor at fencing and dancin[g.] When he graduated, in 1784, at the end of five a[nd] one half years of study, his final report noted that h[is] conduct throughout had been "perfectly regular[,"] and he was recommended for further training.

Having decided on a career in the artillery (the be[st] choice for a young man with mathematical aptitude[),] Napoleon went on to the prestigious École Militai[re] in Paris, where he successfully completed the cour[se] of study—normally two or three years long—in a si[n]gle year. Perhaps the most important lesson taught [at] the École Militaire was that it paid to be a goo[d] royalist. The students, many of them from impecu[n]ious families and fresh from the Spartan regime [of] boarding schools like Brienne, were given priva[te] rooms, sumptuous meals, three clean shirts a wee[k,] and the services of a private hairdresser. Such luxuri[es] were meant to impress the cadets with the potenti[al] rewards of a successful military career, but Napoleo[n,] at least for the present, refused to be seduced. His tru[e] feelings were confided to his notebook in the form [of] an essay entitled "Lament of a Young Patriot Abse[nt] from His Country," which scathingly contrasted "e[f]feminite moderns" with the Corsican heroes of Paoli['s] heyday, "who were enemies of tyranny, of luxur[y,] [and] of vile courtiers."

The young man who expressed these explosive se[n]timents was commissioned a second lieutenant in th[e] French army in September 1785, but his future w[as] far from certain. His formal education complete[d,] Napoleon still engaged in a passionate search for h[is]

The Revolution that had been born in Paris provoked bitter divisions in the provinces. Brittany became a center of Catholic and conservative resistance. Top left and below near right, scenes in Brittany. The plains of the Vendée (above right) witnessed a number of royalist insurrections, and the Vien[ne] valley (center left) experienc[ed] anti-Revolutionary riots [in] 1793. Support for the new r[e]gime came from the southwest[ern] provinces, including Pér[i]gord (bottom left), and t[he] Pas-de-Calais region in t[he] north (below far right).

APPLICATION AND APPRAISAL FORM
Reference: APGR 690-6

EMPLOYEE'S NAME GRAPER Brad Phillip   MPA NO. XA103-88

SKAP TITLE: Ability to orally coordinate and present command positions.

---

1. **Experience:** (Please state when, where, and what tasks you have performed which show you have the knowledge, skill or ability required.)

Prepared a series of five briefings on Ordnance School doctrinal and materiel developments; presented the briefings numerous times over a five day period at the Progress in Logistics 85 exposition. Audiences included groups of general officers up to the three star level. Prepared and presented a briefing to MG Potts outlining my plan for testing a new type maintenance tent; the plan was approved. Prepared a briefing detailing the Vehicle Support Kit concept and evaluation; presented it to MG Salomon and to a group of general officers and senior civilians during the Ordnance Conference. Prepared and presented a briefing on the OC&S position supporting the "FUCHS" NBC Reconnaissance Vehicle to BG Kastenmeyer. Prepared and presented numerous other briefings on Ordnance School issues and positions to senior officers and civilians from other TRADOC organizations, HQ DA, AMC, and test agencies. I normally gave such briefings during coordination meetings and working group meetings. I attended coordination, working group and management team meetings several times a month at other TRADOC organizations, test agencies and AMC commands for materiel systems I managed.

2. **Education/Training:** (Describe education or training you have received which demonstrates your ability in the area required. Please give dates of attendance and name of school.)

Armor Officer Advanced Course, Jul 81 - Feb 82. Intensive training in development and presentation of briefings and in leading discussions. Very intensive training on oral presentation of operational and intelligence estimates for command decisions and planning.
Effective Briefing Techniques, Apr 86. Comprehensive training in preparation and presentation of briefings.

3. **Awards:** (Describe only those awards which demonstrate your ability in the area required.

Commandant's List, Armor Officer Advanced Course, Feb 82 (General Officer Letter of Commendation); Army Achievement Medal, Jul 85

Supervisory Appraisal of Demonstrated Performance	SUPERIOR	ABOVE AVERAGE	AVERAGE	BARELY ACCEPTABLE	NOT OBSERVED
	✓				

COMMENTS: *Confident, articulate, masterful presentations of complex topics — exemplary.*

APPLICATION AND APPRAISAL FORM
Reference: APGR 690-6

EMPLOYEE'S NAME GRAPER Brad Phillip   MPA NO. XA103-88

SKAP TITLE: Ability to write reports, briefing material, and prepare instructions
on intelligence matters.

1. Experience: (Please state when, where, and what tasks you have performed which show you have the knowledge, skill or ability required.)

I have prepared reports and/or briefing materials several times a month continuously for the last three years. I travel every month to joint working groups, management team meetings and program reviews for the materiel systems I manage. I frequently prepare either a briefing or information paper for the meetings; I also prepare a report on every meeting I attend detailing important results and/or issues from the meeting. Other major reports/briefings I prepared include: A report and a briefing to MG Salomon and GEN Otis on my comparison of the mission profiles of the recovery vehicle and the M1 tank; a report to MG Salomon on the projected force structure impact of fielding the Forward Area Air Defense System; an Independent Evaluation Report on a test I planned on a new maintenance tent; and an Independent Evaluation Report and several briefings (up to 2-star level) on a field repair kit for trucks. As a commander and tactical planner, I have: prepared operational concept briefings and intelligence estimates; prepared instructions on collection of intelligence; and developed Essential Elements of Information.

2. Education/Training: (Describe education or training you have received which demonstrates your ability in the area required. Please give dates of attendance and name of school.)

Armor Officer Basic Course, Oct 77 - Jan 78. Training on preparation and presentation of operational concepts and plans briefings, and on use of organic intelligence collection assets. Armor Officer Advanced Course, Jul 81 - Feb 82. Intensive training on preparation of briefings and plans, preparation of intelligence estimates, preparation of intelligence collection plans and instructions, and the preparation of written reports or plans. Effective Briefing Techniques, April 86. Comprehensive training in preparation and presentation of briefings.

3. Awards: (Describe only those awards which demonstrate your ability in the area required.)
Commandant's List, Armor Officer Advanced Course, Feb 82 (General Officer Letter of Commendation); Army Achievement Medal, Jul 85

Supervisory Appraisal of Demonstrated Performance	SUPERIOR	ABOVE AVERAGE	AVERAGE	BARELY ACCEPTABLE	NOT OBSERVED
	✓				

COMMENTS: Habitually complete, correct, clear, concise.
Superb caliber of work reflects thoughtful, careful thorough preparation

EAP FORM 1166a, 1 Jul 82 Edition of 1 Nov 79 is Obsolete

EMPLOYEE'S NAME GRAPER Brad Phillip   MPA NO. XA103-88

SKAP TITLE: Knowledge of military materiel acquisition process to insure that effective

and timely threat support is provided to R&D programs.

---

1. Experience: (Please state when, where, and what tasks you have performed which show you have the knowledge, skill or ability required.)

I have over three years experience in the military materiel acquisition process in combat developments, planning the development, logistics support, acquisition and fielding of military materiel. I am involved with materiel systems throughout their life cycles, from tech base activities through production and deployment. I write and review requirements and concepts for new materiel systems (Operational & Organizational Plans and Required Operational Capabilities). I write and review logistics supportability planning documents (Integrated Logistics Support Plans, Logistics Support Analysis Plans, System MANPRINT Management Plans, and Materiel Fielding Plans). I also develop criteria and plans for testing new materiel or concepts. I frequently coordinate with and have worked closely with TACOM, Night Vision Labs, Natick R&D Center, MICOM and the Chemical RD&E Center to develop new military materiel. I have personally been involved with the following tanks, armored fighting vehicles and field artillery: the M1A1 tank, the Armored Gun System, the Improved Recovery Vehicle, the Forward Area Air Defense System, the M109A2 howitzer, and the M113 Armored Personnel Carrier. I wrote the Ordnance School input into the DA Long Range Research Development and Acquisition Plan and the AMC Materiel Acquisition Management Plan.

2. Education/Training: (Describe education or training you have received which demonstrates your ability in the area required. Please give dates of attendance and name of school.)

Combat Development Course, U.S.Army Command and General Staff College, June - July 85. Comprehensive training in all facets of combat developments in the military materiel acquisition process - training, organization, doctrine and materiel development. TRADOC Independent Evaluator's Orientation Course, TRADOC Independent Evaluation Directorate, Mar 85. Detailed training in planning evaluation of materiel systems. Logistics Support Analysis, U.S.Army Logistics Management Center, Nov 85. Detailed training in preparation and evaluation of Logistics Support Analysis Records, which drive all maintenance, maintenance training, tools and repair parts for a materiel system. Integrated Logistics Support Management Techniques in Materiel Acquisition, U.S.Army Logistics Management Center, Mar 86. Comprehensive training in the management and technical activities used to influence operational requirements and system design.

3. Awards: (Describe only those awards which demonstrate your ability in the area required.)

2d in Class, Combat Developer Course, July 85; Honor Graduate, Logistics Support Analysis course, Nov 85; Honor Graduate, Integrated Logistics Support Management Techniques, Mar 86

Supervisory Appraisal of Demonstrated Performance	SUPERIOR	ABOVE AVERAGE	AVERAGE	BARELY ACCEPTABLE	NOT OBSERVED
	✓				

COMMENTS: Superby knowledgeable of both how the system is supposed to work and how to get the system to produce results

EAP FORM 1166a, 1 Jul 82 Edition of 1 Nov 79 is Obsolete

1. Experience: (Please state when, where, and what tasks you have performed which show you have the knowledge, skill or ability required.)

have over ten years experience as an armor officer; I am by definition and experience an expert in tanks and armored fighting vehicles and their employment including field artillery) on the battlefield. I have been a tank platoon leader, support platoon leader, company executive officer, brigade materiel readiness officer, tank battalion maintenance officer, and tank company commander. Prior to coming to APG I spent the entire 7+ years in tank or armored units, using tanks and armored fighting vehicles on a daily basis. I have maintained tanks and armored fighting vehicles, supported them, personally operated them, used them in a tactical environment, and planned their use. I have also planned and frequently practiced the destruction of Warsaw Pact tanks, armored fighting vehicles, and field artillery. As a tank platoon leader and as a company commander I have planned the use of field artillery, and worked closely with them in field exercises. As a support platoon leader and brigade assistant S-4 I also planned for field artillery supply and support. I have spent the last 3+ years at APG planning the development, acquisition and support of tanks, armored fighting vehicles, and field artillery for the Army.

2. Education/Training: (Describe education or training you have received which demonstrates your ability in the area required. Please give dates of attendance and name of school.) Armor Officer Basic Course, U.S. Army Armor School Oct 77 - Jan 78. Intensive training in operation and maintenance of tanks; also in employment of tanks, armored fighting vehicles and field artillery. Included training in Warsaw Pact vehicles and their employment. Motor Officer Course, U.S. Army Armor School Jan 78 - Mar 78. Detailed training in maintenance operations for tanks, armored fighting vehicles and field artillery. Armor Officer Advanced Course, Jul 81 - Feb 82. Intensive training in operation, maintenance and logistics support of tanks and armored fighting vehicles; very intensive training in employment of tanks, armored fighting vehicles and field artillery, to include Warsaw Pact. Intensive training in preparation of intelligence estimates. Also trained in relative vulnerability of U.S. and Warsaw Pact vehicles. Maintenance Management Officer Course, USAOC&S, Jan 85 - Feb 85. Training in maintenance management and logistics and maintenance operations for all Army vehicles.

3. Awards: (Describe only those awards which demonstrate your ability in the area required.)

2d Bn 81st Armor Certificate of Achievement, Aug 78; Army Commendation Medal, June 81; General Officer Letter of Commendation (Commandant's List Armor Officer Advanced Course), Feb 82; Army Achievement Medal, Jul 85.

Supervisory Appraisal of Demonstrated Performance	SUPERIOR	ABOVE AVERAGE	AVERAGE	BARELY ACCEPTABLE	NOT OBSERVED
	✓				

COMMENTS:

An absolute expert that provides the best from first hand field experience and an in-depth understanding of the business

APPLICATION AND APPRAISAL FORM
Reference: APGR 690-6

GRAPER Brad Phillip
APPLICANT'S NAME

XA103-88
MERIT PROMOTION ANNOUNCEMENT NO.

USAOC&S
ATSL-CD-RE
Dir of Cbt Dev   BR&E
ORG   DIV   BR

Intelligence Research Specialist, GS-132-12
TITLE, SERIES AND GRADE OF VACANCY

3148   278-2434/3254
BLDG. NO.   PHONE

Recovery and Evacuation
Project Officer   CPT, Armor
TITLE, SERIES, GRADE

INSTRUCTIONS TO APPLICANT: Complete all information requested above. For each SKAP listed
in the announcement a separate page (EAP Form 1166a) must be prepared, identifying the SKAP
by title and describing your experience, education/training and awards which shows that you
possess the particular knowledge, skill or ability cited in the SKAP. Your description
should show what, when and where you acquired the knowledge, skill or ability. Your
completed form must be submitted to your first line supervisor (or in his absence, the
second line supervisor) for completion of the appraisal portion. The application must be
completed by both the employee and the supervisor in sufficient time to be received in
the RECRUITMENT AND PLACEMENT DIVISION, CIVILIAN PERSONNEL OFFICE, BUILDING 305, by the
closing date of the announcement.

INSTRUCTIONS TO SUPERVISOR: Read the title and definition of appropriate SKAP and select
one of four adjective ratings provided under demonstrated performance. If you have not
observed performance relevent to this SKAP, mark NOT OBSERVED. You are reminded that
when evaluating employees, as a minimum, you must do so based upon observation of the
employee's performance, characteristics, work habits, and related attitudes. Comments
relative to each SKAP are required.

RATING DEFINITIONS:
SUPERIOR: Continually EXCEEDS performance standards/requirements in this SKAP.
ABOVE AVERAGE: Frequently EXCEEDS performance standards/requirements in this SKAP.
AVERAGE: Continually MEETS performance standards/requirements in this SKAP.
BARELY ACCEPTABLE: Occasionally MEETS performance standards/requirements in this SKAP.

CERTIFICATION: We certify that the information submitted is accurate.

_____ 1 Apr 88   _____ LTC 1 April 88
EMPLOYEE'S SIGNATURE AND DATE   SUPERVISOR'S SIGNATURE AND DATE

EAP FORM 1166, 1 Jul 82 Edition of 1 Nov 79 isObsolete

Mar 1985	40 Hrs	TRADOC Independent Evaluator's Orientation Course	TRADOC Independent Evaluation Directorate Ft. Leavenworth, KS	Cert.
Feb 1985	240 Hrs	Maintenance Management Officer's Course	U.S.Army Ordnance Center & School, APG, MD	Diploma
Feb 1982	1040 Hrs	Armor Officer Advanced Course	U.S.Army Armor School Ft. Knox, KY	Diploma
Mar 1978	640 Hrs	Motor Officer Course	U.S.Army Armor School Ft. Knox, KY	Diploma
Jan 1978	960 Hrs	Armor Officer Basic Course	U.S.Army Armor School Ft. Knox, KY	Diploma

Place an "X" in the proper column for each question below.

	YES	NO

38 Are you a citizen of the United States? If "NO", write the country or countries you are a citizen of: _____ **[X YES]**

> **Important note about questions 39 through 44:** We will consider the date, facts, and circumstances of each event you list. In most cases you can still be considered for Federal jobs. However, if you fail to tell the truth or fail to list all relevant events, this failure may be grounds for not hiring you, for firing you after you begin work, or for criminal prosecution [18 USC 1001].

39 During the last **10 years**, were you **fired from any job** for any reason, did you quit **after being told that** you would be fired, or did you leave by mutual agreement because of specific problems? If "YES", use 47 to write for each job: a) *the name of the employer,* b) *the approximate date you left the job,* and c) *the reason(s) why you left* ..... **[X NO]**

> **When answering questions 40 through 44 you may omit:** 1) traffic fines of $100.00 or less; 2) any violation of law committed before your 18th birthday, if finally decided in juvenile court or under a youth offender law; 3) any conviction set aside under the Federal Youth Corrections Act or similar State law; 4) any conviction whose record was expunged under Federal or State law.

40 Have you **ever** been convicted of or forfeited collateral for **any felony?** ..... **[X NO]**

A felony is defined as any violation of law punishable by imprisonment of longer than one year, except for violations called misdemeanors under State law which are punishable by imprisonment of two years or less.

41 Have you **ever** been convicted of or forfeited collateral for any **firearms** or **explosives** violation? ..... **[X NO]**

42 During the last **10 years** have you forfeited collateral, been convicted, been imprisoned, been on probation, or been on parole? Do **not** include violations reported in 40 or 41 above ..... **[X NO]**

43 Are you **now** under charges for **any** violation of law? ..... **[X NO]**

44 Have you **ever** been convicted by a **court-martial?** If no military service, answer "NO" ..... **[X NO]**

> **IF YOU ANSWERED "YES" TO 40, 41, 42, 43, or 44, GIVE DETAILS IN 47.** For each violation write the: 1) date; 2) charge; 3) place; 4) court; and 5) action taken.

45 Do any of your relatives work for the United States Government or the United States Armed Forces? Include: *father; mother; husband; wife; son; daughter; brother; sister; uncle; aunt; first cousin; nephew; niece; father-in-law; mother-in-law; son-in-law; daughter-in-law; brother-in-law; sister-in-law; stepfather; stepmother; stepson; stepdaughter; stepbrother; stepsister; half brother;* and *half sister* ..... **[X NO]**

If "YES", use 47 to write for each of these relatives, their: a) *name;* b) *relationship;* c) *department, agency, or branch of the Armed Forces.*

46 Do you receive, or have you ever applied for retirement pay, pension, or other pay based on military, Federal civilian, or District of Columbia Government service? ..... **[X NO]**

47 Write the number to which each answer applies. **If you need more space,** use sheets of paper the same size as this page. On each sheet write your name, Social Security Number, and the announcement number or job title. Attach all additional sheets at the top of page 3.

32. Already have SECRET clearance.

YOU MUST SIGN THIS APPLICATION. Read the following carefully before you sign.

A false statement on any part of your application may be grounds for not hiring you, or for firing you after you begin work. Also, you may be punished by fine or imprisonment (U.S. Code, Title 18, Section 1001).

I **understand** that any information I give may be investigated as allowed by law or Presidential order;

I **consent** to the release of information about my ability and fitness for Federal employment by *employers, schools, law enforcement agencies and other individuals and organizations,* to *investigators, personnel staffing specialists, and other authorized employees of the Federal Government.*

I **certify** that, to the best of my knowledge and belief, **all** of my statements are true, correct, complete, and made in good faith.

48 SIGNATURE *(Sign each application in dark ink)*

49 DATE SIGNED *(Month, day, year)*

March 28, 1988

Page 4

EDUCATION

25 Did you graduate from high school? *If you have a GED high school equivalency or will graduate within the next nine months, answer "YES".*

YES [X] If "YES", give month and year of graduation: __May 1972__

NO [ ] If "NO", give the highest grade you completed: _____

26 Write the name and location *(city and state)* of the last high school you attended

Crown Point High School, Crown Point, IN

27 Have you ever attended college or graduate school?   YES [X] If "YES", continue with **28**.   NO [ ] If "NO", go to **31**.

28 NAME AND LOCATION *(city, state and ZIP code)* OF COLLEGE OR UNIVERSITY. *If you expect to graduate within nine months, give the month and year you expect to receive your degree.*

	MONTH AND YEAR ATTENDED From	To	NO. OF CREDITS COMPLETED Semester Hours OR Quarter Hours	TYPE OF DEGREE *(e.g. B.A., M.A.)*	YEAR OF DEGREE
1) Morehead State University, Morehead, KY	Aug 72	May 73	34		
2) Indiana University, Bloomington, IN	Aug 74	Aug 77		B.A.	1977
3)					

29

CHIEF UNDERGRADUATE SUBJECTS *Show major on the first line*	NO. OF CREDITS COMPLETED Semester Hours OR Quarter Hours
1) History	42
2) Military Science	16
3)	

30

CHIEF GRADUATE SUBJECTS *Show major on the first line*	NO. OF CREDITS COMPLETED Semester Hours OR Quarter Hours
1)	
2)	
3)	

31 Have you completed any other courses or training related to the kind of jobs you are applying for *(for example, trade, vocational, Armed Forces, or business)?*   YES [ ]   NO [ ]
If "YES", give the information requested below. *(More courses?—Use a sheet of paper)*
If "NO", go to **32**.

MONTH AND YEAR TRAINING COMPLETED	TOTAL CLASSROOM HOURS	SUBJECT(S)	NAME AND LOCATION OF SCHOOL *(City, state, and ZIP code, if known)*	CERTIFICATE, DIPLOMA, etc. *(if any)*
1) Mar 1986	80	Integrated Logistics Spt. Mgmt. Techniques	U.S. Army Logistics Management Center Fort Lee, VA	Cert.
2) Nov 1985	80	Logistics Support Analysis	U.S. Army Logistics Management Center Fort Lee, VA	Cert.
3) July 1985	160	Combat Developments	U.S. Army Command & General Staff College Fort Leavenworth, KS	Cert.

SPECIAL SKILLS, ACCOMPLISHMENTS AND AWARDS

32 List your special qualifications, skills or accomplishments that may help you get a job. *Some examples are: skills with machines; most important publications (do not submit copies); public speaking and writing experience; membership in professional or scientific societies; patents or inventions; etc.*

Thorough knowledge of the Military Materiel Acquisition Process, Combat Developments, and Integrated Logistics Support. Extensive knowledge of tanks, armored fighting vehicles, and field artillery. Extensive knowledge of U.S. and Warsaw Pact employment doctrine. Knowledge through field experience and Armor Advanced Course in preparation of intelligence estimates.

33 How many words per minute can you: TYPE? | TAKE DICTATION?

Agencies may test your skills before hiring you.

34 List job-related licenses or certificates that you have, such as: *registered nurse; lawyer; radio operator; driver's; pilot's; etc.*

LICENSE OR CERTIFICATE	DATE OF LATEST LICENSE OR CERTIFICATE	STATE OR OTHER LICENSING AGENCY
1)		
2)		

35 Do you speak or read a language other than English *(include sign language)?* *Applicants for jobs that require a language other than English may be given an interview conducted solely in that language.*   YES [ ]   NO [X]
If "YES", list each language and place an "X" in each column that applies to you.
If "NO", go to **36**

LANGUAGE(S)	CAN PREPARE AND GIVE LECTURES Fluently	With Difficulty	CAN SPEAK AND UNDERSTAND Fluently	Passably	CAN TRANSLATE ARTICLES Into English	From English	CAN READ ARTICLES FOR OWN USE Easily	With Difficulty
1)								
2)								

36 List any honors, awards, or fellowships you have received. For each, give the year it was received.

Army Commendation Medal 1981
Commandant's List, Armor Officer Advanced Course, 1982
Army Achievement Medal 1985

REFERENCES

37 List three people who are **not** related to you and who know your qualifications and fitness for the kind of job(s) for which you are applying. **Do not** list supervisors you listed under **24**.

FULL NAME OF REFERENCE	PRESENT BUSINESS OR HOME ADDRESS *(Number, street, city, state, and ZIP code)*	TELEPHONE NUMBER(S) *(Include area code)*	BUSINESS OR OCCUPATION
1) Richard A. Stillman	Directorate of Cbt Developments USAOC&S, ATSL-CD, APG, MD 21005	278-5698	Deputy Director
2) Cheryl A. Bird	1948 Sue Creek Dr., Baltimore, MD	574-2125	Intelligence Research Spec.
3) Joseph A. Masterson	Directorate of Cbt Developments USAOC&S, ATSL-CD-MS, APG, MD	278-3375	Chief, Materiel Logistics Syste

Standard Form 171-A—Continuation Sheet for SF 171

Form Approved:
OMB No. 3206-001

• Attach all SF 171-A's to your application at the top of page 3.

1. Name (Last, First, Middle)	2. Social Security Number
GRAPER Brad Phillip	303 62 6929

3. Job Title or Announcement Number You Are Applying For	4. Date Completed
Intelligence Research Specialist XA103-88	28 March 1988

ADDITIONAL WORK EXPERIENCE BLOCKS IF NEEDED

☐ Name and address of employer's organization (include ZIP Code, if known)	Dates employed (give month and year)	Average number of hours per week
Headquarters and Headquarters Company 2d Battalion 81st Armor 1st Armored Division Erlangen, Germany APO NY 09066	From Mar 79 To June 80	60

	Salary or earnings	Place of employment
	Starting $ per Ending $ per	City Erlangen State FRG

Exact title of your job	Your immediate supervisor		Number and job titles of any employees you supervised
Support Platoon Leader	Name CPT Smith	Area Code Telephone Number	29 truck drivers

Kind of business or organization (manufacturing, accounting, social service, etc.)	If Federal employment (civilian or military) list series, grade or rank, and the date of your last promotion	Your reason for leaving
U.S. Army	1st Lieutenant, September 1979	Job Advancement

Description of work: Describe your specific duties, responsibilities and accomplishments in this job. If you describe more than one type of work (for example, carpentry and painting or personnel and budget), write the approximate percentage of time you spent doing each.

I was the Support Platoon Leader and Assistant S-4 (Logistics Officer) for a tank battalion in an armored division. I was resposible for supervision, operations and maintenace of a 29 man support platoon with 17 trucks. I was also responsible for all battalion fuel and ammunition planning, requisitioning, operations and accountability. I planned and supervised all ammunition and fuel resupply for the tank battalion through three major and numerous minor tactical field exercises and three tank gunneries. Despite severe shortages in personnel and aging equipment, the platoon accomplished its mission in a timely and expeditious manner 100% of the time. I am very familiar with the Army supply system; I routinely coordinated with the Division Ammunition Office and the Supply and Services Battalion to accomplish resupply of fuel and ammunition. In addition, I planned and accomplished the replacement of the entire battalion basic load of tank ammunition (approximately 3000 rounds

For Agency Use (skill codes, etc.)

☐ Name and address of employer's organization (include ZIP Code, if known)	Dates employed (give month and year)	Average number of hours per week
C Company 2d Battalion 81st Armor 1st Armored Division Erlangen, Germany APO NY 09066	From: Apr 78 To Mar 79	60

	Salary or earnings	Place of employment
	Starting $ per Ending $ per	City Erlangen State FRG

Exact title of your job	Your immediate supervisor		Number and job titles of any employees you supervised
Tank Platoon Leader	Name CPT Westholm	Area Code Telephone Number	23 tank crewmen

Kind of business or organization (manufacturing, accounting, social service, etc.)	If Federal employment (civilian or military), list series, grade or rank, and the date of your last promotion	Your reason for leaving
U.S. Army	2d Lieutenant, August 1977	Job Advancement

Description of work: Describe your specific duties, responsibilities and accomplishments in this job. If you describe more than one type of work (for example, carpentry and painting or personnel and budget), write the approximate percentage of time you spent doing each.

I was a tank platoon leader in a tank battalion in an armored division. I was responsible for the training, welfare, employment and discipline of a 23 man tank platoon equipped with six M60A1 tanks. I planned and lead tank crew training in maintenance, tactics and gunnery. I also ensured that all crewmen were thoroughly up to date on Warsaw Pact vehicles, tactics and doctrine. My platoon was continually rated as one of the best in the battalion in field exercises, and was in the top 25% of all the platoons in the 1st Armored Division in gunnery. This was due to good maintenance, good tactics, and excellent training and motivation in the platoon.

For Agency Use (skill codes, etc.)

THE FEDERAL GOVERNMENT

Standard Form 171-A—Continuation Sheet for SF 171

Form Approved:
OMB No. 3206-001

• Attach all SF 171-A's to your application at the top of page 3.

1. Name (Last, First, Middle)	2. Social Security Number
GRAPER Brad Phillip	303 62 6929

3. Job Title or Announcement Number You Are Applying For	4. Date Completed
Intelligence Research Specialist XA103-88	28 March 88

ADDITIONAL WORK EXPERIENCE BLOCKS IF NEEDED

Name and address of employer's organization (include ZIP Code, if known)	Dates employed (give month and year)	Average number of hours per week
Headquarters, 1st Brigade 1st Infantry Division Fort Riley, KS	From: Feb 82 To: Dec 82	60

	Salary or earnings	Place of employment
	Starting $ per Ending $ per	City Ft. Riley State KS

Exact title of your job	Your immediate supervisor		Number and job titles of any employees you supervised
Assistant S-4	Name MAJ Bishop	Area Code Telephone Number	

Kind of business or organization (manufacturing, accounting, social service, etc.)	If Federal employment (civilian or military), list series, grade or rank, and the date of your last promotion	Your reason for leaving
U.S. Army	Captain, May 1981	Job Advancement

Description of work: Describe your specific duties, responsibilities and accomplishments in this job. If you describe more than one type of work (for example carpentry and painting or personnel and budget), write the approximate percentage of time you spent doing each

I was Assistant Brigade S-4 (Logistics Officer) and Brigade Materiel Readiness Officer for an armored brigade of two tank battalions and two mechanized infantry battalions. I compiled the brigade Materiel Status Report and Unit Status Report (sent to HQ DA) on a monthly basis, and coordinated on a daily basis with the division maintenance battalion for support. I was the maintenance management inspector for the brigade, and the administrative movements and transportation officer. I personally planned and managed the turn-in of M113 antitank guided missile carriers for the brigade. I also planned, coordinated and managed the lateral transfer and cross leveling of equipment within the brigade. As brigade transportation officer, I procured equipment for and coordinated the transportation for the annual evaluati of the 32d Separate Infantry Brigade.

For Agency Use (skill codes, etc.)

Name and address of employer's organization (include ZIP Code, if known)	Dates employed (give month and year)	Average number of hours per week
Headquarters and Headquarters Company 2d Brigade 1st Armored Division Erlangen, Germany APO NY 09066	From: June 80 To: June 81	60

	Salary or earnings	Place of employment
	Starting $ per Ending $ per	City Erlangen State FRG

Exact title of your job	Your immediate supervisor		Number and job titles of any employees you supervised
Executive Officer Headquarters Company	Name CPT Spears	Area Code Telephone Number	12 mechanics

Kind of business or organization (manufacturing, accounting, social service, etc.)	If Federal employment (civilian or military), list series, grade or rank, and the date of your last promotion	Your reason for leaving
U.S. Army	Captain, May 1981	Advanced Schooling

Description of work: Describe your specific duties, responsibilities and accomplishments in this job. If you describe more than one type of work (for example, carpentry and painting or personnel and budget), write the approximate percentage of time you spent doing each.

I was the Executive Officer of a brigade headquarters company in an armored division. I was responsible for the training and performance of a 12 man maintenance team, and for the maintenance of 32 tracked and wheeled vehicles. I planned and supervised maintenance operations, mess operations, supply operations, and maintenance and drivers training for the brigade headquarters. I also forecasted, requisitioned and ensured proper storage of all training and basic load ammunition for the company. In addition I was the security officer, property officer, arms room officer, and Nuclear, Biological and Chemical officer for the company. I improved the company repair parts operation, supply accountability, mess operations, NBC equipment, weapons and maintenance through a thorough inspection and fault correction program. I also initiated a training program which greatly improved the personal weap qualification scores and NBC capabilities of the company.

For Agency Use (skill codes,

Standard Form 171-A—Continuation Sheet for SF 171

Form Approved:
OMB No. 3206-0012

• Attach all SF 171-A's to your application at the top of page 3.

1. Name (Last, First, Middle)	2. Social Security Number
GRAPER Brad Phillip	303 62 6929

3. Job Title or Announcement Number You Are Applying For	4. Date Completed
Intelligence Research Specialist XA103-88	28 March 1988

ADDITIONAL WORK EXPERIENCE BLOCKS IF NEEDED

Name and address of employer's organization (include ZIP Code if known)	Dates employed (give month and year)	Average number of hours per week
1st Battalion 34th Armor 1st Infantry Division Fort Riley, KS	From: June 83 To: Dec 84	60

Salary or earnings — Starting $ per — Ending $ per

Place of employment — City Ft. Riley — State KS

Exact title of your job	Your immediate supervisor		Number and job titles of any employees you supervised
Commander, B Company	Name LTC Williams	Area Code Telephone Number	72 officers, tank crewmen and mechanics

Kind of business or organization (manufacturing, accounting, social service, etc.)	If Federal employment (civilian or military), list series, grade or rank, and the date of your last promotion	Your reason for leaving
U.S. Army	Captain, May 1981	Advanced Schooling

Description of work. Describe your specific duties, responsibilities and accomplishments in this job. *If you describe more than one type of work (for example, carpentry and painting, or personnel and budget), write the approximate percentage of time you spent doing each.*

I was the commander of a 72 man tank company equipped with 14 M60A1 tanks and six other vehicles. I was responsible for the training, discipline, welfare, readiness and employment of the company. I planned and supervised all training and maintenance. I personally gave instruction in U.S. and Warsaw Pact weapons systems characteristics, employment doctrine and tactics in both offense and defense, employment of artillery and mortars, night operations, small arms and maintenance. In particular I emphasized tactics and quick analysis of the Threat and the tactical situation. The results of this training were evident in the considerable tactical success the company enjoyed both at Ft. Irwin and at Ft. Riley. In addition, the maintenance policies and procedures I established were proven effective by the above average readiness of the company's tanks.

For Agency Use (skill codes, etc.)

Name and address of employer's organization (include ZIP Code, if known)	Dates employed (give month and year)	Average number of hours per week
1st Battalion 34th Armor 1st Infantry Division Fort Riley, KS	From: Dec 82 To: June 83	60

Salary or earnings — Starting $ per — Ending $ per

Place of employment — City Ft. Riley — State KS

Exact title of your job	Your immediate supervisor		Number and job titles of any employees you supervised
Battalion Maintenance Officer	Name MAJ Justice	Area Code Telephone Number	99 mechanics

Kind of business or organization (manufacturing, accounting, social service, etc.)	If Federal employment (civilian or military), list series, grade or rank, and the date of your last promotion	Your reason for leaving
U.S. Army	Captain, May 1981	Job Advancement

Description of work: Describe your specific duties, responsibilities and accomplishments in this job. *If you describe more than one type of work (for example, carpentry and painting, or personnel and budget), write the approximate percentage of time you spent doing each.*

I was the Battalion Maintenance Officer of a tank battalion equipped with 54 M60A1 tanks and 80+ other vehicles. I lead and supervised a 99 man maintenance platoon responsible for maintenance of the battalion's 130+ vehicles. I planned, organized and supervised the battalion's maintenance operations, and coordinated daily with the forward support maintenance company for support. I also planned and coordinated training for the mechanics in the platoon. I wrote the battalion's Standard Operating Procedures for maintenance, and reorganized the maintenance platoon to conform to the new Table of Organization and Equipment. I improved the Oil Analysis and repair parts programs in the battalion, and successfully executed the job performance skills testing of all tank turret mechanics in the 1st Infantry Division. Through continuous coordination and effective management of maintenance resources I brought the battalion's operational availability up to an average over 95%.

For Agency Use (skill codes, etc.)

PREVIOUS EDITION USABLE   NSN 7540-00-935-7157   171-205

Standard Form 171-A (Rev. 2/84)
Office of Personnel Management
FPM Chapter 295

23 May we ask your present employer about your character, qualifications and work record? A "NO" will not affect our review of your qualifications. If you answer "NO" and we need to contact your present employer before we can offer you a job, we will contact you first . . . .

YES	NO
	X

- INCLUDE VOLUNTEER WORK (non-paid work)—if the work (or a part of the work) is like the job you are applying for, complete all parts of the experience block just as you would for a paying job. You may receive credit for work experience with religious, community, welfare, service, and other organizations.

24 READ **WORK EXPERIENCE** ON THE INSTRUCTION PAGE BEFORE YOU BEGIN

- Describe your current or most recent job in Block **A** and work backwards, describing each job you held **during the past 10 years.**
- You may sum up in one block work that you did **more than 10 years ago.** But, if that work **is related** to the type of job you are applying for, describe each related job in a separate block.
- If you were **unemployed** for longer than **3 months,** list the dates and your address(es) at that time in **47.** Do **not** list unemployment that was more than 10 years ago.

- INCLUDE MILITARY SERVICE—You should complete all parts of the experience block just as you would for a non-military job, including all supervisory experience. Describe each major change of duties or responsibilities in a separate experience block.
- IF YOU NEED MORE EXPERIENCE BLOCKS OR MORE SPACE TO DESCRIBE A JOB— For more blocks, use the SF 171-A or sheets of paper the same size as this page (be sure to include all information we ask for in **A** or **B** below). On **each** sheet show your name, Social Security Number, and the announcement number or job title. **For more space** continue in **47** or on a sheet of paper as described above.
- IF YOU NEED TO UPDATE (ADD MORE RECENT JOBS), use the SF 172 or a sheet of paper as described above.

A Name and address of employer's organization *(include ZIP Code, if known)*
TRADOC Battlefield Recovery & Evacuation Ofc.
U.S.Army Ordnance Center and School
ATTN: ATSL-CD-RE
Aberdeen Proving Ground, MD 21005-5201

Dates employed *(give month and year)*
From: 1 Dec 87 To: present

Salary or earnings
Starting $ per
Ending $ per

Average number of hours per week
55

Place of employment
City Aberdeen Proving Grnd
State MD

Exact title of your job
Recovery & Evacuation
Project Officer

Your immediate supervisor
Name LTC Cizmadia
Area Code 301 Telephone Number 278 2434

Number and job titles of any employees you supervise(d)

Kind of business or organization *(manufacturing, accounting, social service, etc.)* U.S. Army
Ordnance Center & School

If Federal employment *(civilian or military)*, list: series, grade or rank, and the date of your last promotion
Captain, May 1981

Your reason for wanting to leave
Leaving active duty

Description of work: Describe your specific duties, responsibilities and accomplishments in this job. *If you describe more than one type of work (for example, carpentry and painting, or personnel and budget), write the approximate percentage of time you spent doing each.* I plan, coordinate and manage the development and acquisition of armored recovery vehicles for the Army. I perform individual research, collect, assemble and analyze pertinent facts, and prepare recommendations and clear, concise reports to the general officer (up to 4-star) level. This also includes writing general officer level correspondence. In addition, I prepare and give briefings to general officers or their representatives. I routinely review and evaluate required new vehicle characteristics as stated in Required Operational Capability (ROC) documents, using my extensive knowledge of employment doctrine and tactics and a thorough understanding of military science. I then formulate and coordinate appropriate changes with other TRADOC organizations, AMC, private industry, and HQ DA. I review and evaluate logistics support planning for recovery vehicles, and formulate and coordinate changes. I also write and coordinate new recovery doctrine; this requires review and analysis of previous U.S. and NATO doctrine and analysis of new Threat doctrine.

For Agency Use (skill codes, etc.)

B Name and address of employer's organization *(include ZIP Code, if known)*
Directorate of Combat Developments
U.S.Army Ordnance Center and School
ATTN: ATSL-CD-MS
Aberdeen Proving Ground, MD 21005-5201

Dates employed *(give month and year)*
From: Feb 85 To: Dec 87

Salary or earnings
Starting $ per
Ending $ per

Average number of hours per week
55 - 60

Place of employment
City Aberdeen Proving Grnd
State MD

Exact title of your job
Senior Staff Officer & Chief,
Logistics Systems Branch

Your immediate supervisor
Name MAJ Leibel
Area Code 301 Telephone Number 278 3375

Number and job titles of any employees you supervised
13 Project/Staff Officer

Kind of business or organization *(manufacturing, accounting, social service, etc.)* U.S. Army
Ordnance Center and School

If Federal employment *(civilian or military)*, list series, grade or rank, and the date of your last promotion
Captain, May 1981

Your reason for leaving
Personnel Realignment

Description of work: Describe your specific duties, responsibilities and accomplishments in this job. *If you describe more than one type of work (for example, carpentry and painting, or personnel and budget), write the approximate percentage of time you spent doing each.* I supervised 13 military and civilian staff/project officers in planning and managing the development, acquisition, and Integrated Logistics Support (ILS) of 165 different vehicles and materiel systems. I directed and coordinated the research, planning, and overall effort of the branch, and reviewed all briefings, reports, and analyses produced. In addition, I planned and/or coordinated the ILS of these important weapons systems: the M1 tank, the Armored Gun System and the Forward Area Air Defense System. I am thoroughly familiar with the military materiel acquisition process. I am also thoroughly familiar with U.S. weapons systems and their vulnerabilities, having used this knowledge to pl their support. I have also acted as a subject matter expert on U.S. and Threat employment doctrine; I frequently reviewed and analyzed new doctrine in development and provided recommendations to other TRADOC organizations. I was the interim OC&S Chief of Threat Management during the TRADOC inspection (OC&S did not have a Threat Manager at the time); the inspection results were very favorable.

For Agency Use (skill codes, etc.)

Application for Federal Employment—SF 171

Form Approved: OMB No. 3206-0012

Read the instructions before you complete this application. *Type or print clearly in dark ink.*

GENERAL INFORMATION

1 What kind of job are you applying for? *Give title and announcement number (if any)*

Intelligence Research Specialist XA103-88

2 If the announcement lists several job titles, which jobs are you applying for?

3 Social Security Number

303 | 62 | 6929

4 Birth date *(Month, Day, Year)*

June 26, 1954

5 Name *(Last, First, Middle)*

GRAPER Brad Phillip

Street address or RFD number *(include apartment number, if any)*

600 Yorkshire Drive

City	State	ZIP Code
Edgewood	MD	21040

6 Other names ever used

7 Sex *(for statistical use)*
[X] Male [ ] Female

8 Home Phone

Area Code: 301 Number: 676-6496

9 Work Phone

Area Code: 301 Number: 278-2434 Ext.

10 Were you ever employed as a civilian by the Federal Government? If "NO", go to 11. If "YES", mark each type of job you held with an "X".

[ ] Temporary [ ] Career-Conditional [ ] Career [ ] Excepted

What is your highest grade, classification series and job title?

Dates at highest grade: FROM ___ TO ___

11 Do you have any applications for Federal employment on file with the U.S. Office of Personnel Management? If "NO", mark here [X] and go to 12. If "YES", write below and continue in 47 the information for each application: (a) the name of the office that has your application; (b) the title of the job; (c) the date of your Notice of Results; and (d) your rating.

FOR USE OF EXAMINING OFFICE ONLY

Material	Entered register:
[ ] Submitted	
[ ] Returned	

Notations.

Form reviewed:

Form approved:

Option	Grade	Earned Rating	Preference	Aug. Rating
			[ ] 5 Points (Tent.)	
			[ ] 10 Pts. (30%) Or More Comp. Dis.	
			[ ] 10 Pts. Less Than 30% Comp. Dis.	
			[ ] Other 10 Points	
			[ ] Disallowed	

Initials and Date

[ ] Being Investigated

FOR USE OF APPOINTING OFFICER ONLY

Preference has been verified through proof that the separation was under honorable conditions, and other proof as required.

[ ] 5-Point [ ] 10-Point—30% or More Compensable Disability [ ] 10-Point—Less Than 30% Compensable Disability [ ] 10-Point—Other

Signature and Title

Agency | Date

AVAILABILITY

12 When can you start work? *(Month and Year)*

April 88

13 What is the lowest pay you will accept?

Pay $___ per ___ OR Grade GS-11

14 Are you willing to work:

	YES	NO
A. In the Washington, D.C., metropolitan area?	X	
B. Outside the 50 United States?	X	
C. Any place in the United States?	X	

D. Only in *(list the location[s])*

15 Are you willing to work:

	YES	NO
A. 40 hours per week (full-time)?	X	
B. 25-32 hours per week (part-time)?		X
C. 17-24 hours per week (part-time)?		X
D. 16 or fewer hours per week (part-time)?		X
E. In an intermittent job (on-call/seasonal)?		X
F. Weekends, shifts, or rotating shifts?	X	

16 Are you willing to take a temporary job lasting:

	YES	NO
A. 5 to 12 months (sometimes longer)?	X	
B. 1 to 4 months?		X
C. Less than 1 month?		X

17 Are you willing to travel away from home for:

	YES	NO
A. 1 to 5 nights each month?	X	
B. 6 to 10 nights each month?	X	
C. 11 or more nights each month?	X	

MILITARY SERVICE AND VETERAN PREFERENCE

18 Have you served on active duty in the United States Military Service? If your only active duty was training in the Reserves or National Guard, answer "NO". If "NO", go to 22.

	YES	NO
	X	

19 Were you honorably discharged from the military service? If your discharge was changed to "honorable" or "general" by a Discharge Review Board, answer "YES". If you received a clemency discharge, answer "NO". If "NO", explain in 47.

20 Did you or will you retire at or above the rank of major or lieutenant commander? — X

21 List the dates, branch, and serial number for all active duty service.

FROM	TO	BRANCH OF SERVICE	SERIAL NUMBER
29 Sep 77	present	Army, Armor	303 62 6929

22 Place an "X" in the box next to your Veteran Preference claim. Mark only **one** box. See the instructions for eligibility information.

[X] NO PREFERENCE

[2] 5-POINT PREFERENCE—You must show proof when you are hired.

10-POINT PREFERENCE—If you claim 10-point preference, you must complete a Standard Form 15, which is available at any Federal Job Information Center. ATTACH THE COMPLETED SF 15 TO THIS APPLICATION, TOGETHER WITH THE PROOF REQUESTED IN THE SF 15.

[3] Non-compensably disabled or Purple Heart recipient.

[4] Compensably disabled (less than 30%).

[5] Spouse, widow(er), or mother.

[6] Compensably disabled (30% or more).

bove, the Comte de Mirabeau, a leading ad-
ocate of constitutional monarchy until his
eath in 1791. Above right, the Marquis de
afayette, who fled France in 1792 after try-
ng to save the lives of the royal family. Right,
harles Maurice de Talleyrand-Périgord,
Iapoleon's foreign minister until 1809 and a
rominent figure in French politics through
e 1830s.

fe's direction. He read voraciously, everything from
lato and Plutarch to Rousseau's *Confessions* and con-
emporary works of history. After a year with his reg-
nent he requested leave to visit Corsica, where he
lanned to devote himself to writing a history of his
ative island.

Soon after his arrival in Ajaccio, Napoleon found
imself consumed by family business. The deaths of
Iapoleon's father and great-uncle had incurred a
angle of sizable debts and disagreement about claims
) a mulberry orchard that the Buonapartes managed
nder a government contract. Taking advantage of
ne generous policies of the French army, Napoleon
nanaged to extend his leave for almost two years. In
eptember 1788 he returned to military service at the
own of Auxonne in eastern France. Eleven months
ter, in the wake of popular uprisings and a mutiny
y the common soldiers, he joined the officers of his
egiment in swearing an oath of allegiance to the new
Iational Assembly. The French Revolution was at
and.

King Louis XVI, who came to the throne when
Iapoleon was five years old, had begun his reign
uided by able ministers seeking to reform France's
utmoded legal and financial systems, overhaul the
uilds, and chip away at the privileges enjoyed by

*Facing page, above, the Assembly of the Notables, a pre-
Revolutionary council, rejecting universal taxation in
1787. Facing page, below, the Tennis Court Oath. Denied
their assembly hall, representatives of the Third Estate
(nonprivileged commoners) met on a Versailles tennis
court on June 20, 1789, and swore to remain in session
until France had a written constitution. Above, the Declaration of the Rights of Man and of the Citizen (1789),
"the credo of the new age."*

persons of rank. Notable reforms were achieved in
modernizing the army, especially the artillery. But
stymied by the resistance of the privileged classes to
tax reforms and burdened by debts incurred in the
aftermath of the American Revolution, Louis' government was virtually bankrupt by 1789. With great
misgivings, Louis acceded to demands that he sum-
mon the States-General, the kingdom's representative
assembly, which had not met since 1614.

Elections for the States-General aroused widespread hope, especially among the Third Estate
(nonprivileged commoners). However, the representatives of the First and Second estates (the clergy and
the nobility) were determined to preserve their right
to vote separately from the Third Estate and thus to
block any hostile measures. When it became apparent
that the king supported the clergy and nobles, the

outraged deputies of the Third Estate formed a National Assembly and swore not to disperse until France became a constitutional monarchy. Louis resisted. On July 14, 1789, a Paris mob stormed the royal fortress known as the Bastille, where, it was rumored, forces for a royal coup d'état were being marshaled. Peasant insurrections spread rapidly through the countryside. Louis capitulated by accepting the National Assembly, but in October 1789, after another round of popular violence, he was

brought forcibly from Versailles to Paris. To maintain law and order against threats from both the populace and the king's supporters, the assembly voted to abolish feudal privileges, adopted a declaration of human rights, and recognized the National Guard, which had been formed under the leadership of the Marquis de Lafayette. The first noble émigré, headed by the king's brother, fled to Germany.

Napoleon deplored the spectacles of mutiny and riot that he had witnessed at his post in Auxonne, but he was quick to realize that the events of 1789 offered an opportunity to change Corsica's fortunes for the better. By September of that year he was back in Ajaccio, which was as yet untouched by the developments convulsing the mainland. Napoleon ordered a shipment of the Revolution's tricolor cockades and called on the French governor to authorize their use. The demand touched off an uprising in Paris and led, in short order, to the recall of the exiled Pasquale de Paoli. It was a heady victory for the twenty-year-old patriot, who had all his life idolized Paoli.

Below, the women of Paris armed with pikes, marching on Versailles in October 1789. Sparked by a shortage of bread in the capital, the march ended when the crowds forced the king and queen to abandon the palace and return to Paris. A popular song of the day went "Here comes the banker and here comes the baker's wife. . . . "

Napoleon, along with his elder brother, Joseph, [an]d his younger brother Lucien, assumed that the [B]onaparte family would play a leading role in [Pa]oli's new government. Paoli had other ideas. He [wa]s inclined to believe that Corsica would fare better [as] a British protectorate and was suspicious of the [B]onaparte clan, especially Napoleon, who had [m]anaged to secure a commission as a lieutenant colo[ne]l in the Corsican National Guard. The enmity be[tw]een Napoleon and his old hero sharpened when

Paoli sabotaged Corsican participation in a French expedition against the Sardinian islands of Maddalena and Caprera. Napoleon avoided an open break, but the hot-headed and idealistic Lucien denounced Paoli as a traitor in a letter to revolutionary authorities in the port city of Toulon on the mainland. When an ally of the Buonapartes appeared to demand Paoli's arrest, the Paolist party rallied around its leader. A last-minute attempt by Napoleon to lead an assault against the Paolists' stronghold ended in

Left, Jean Paul Marat, Georges Jacques Danton, and Maximilien Robespierre, three leaders of the Jacobins. The Jacobins were radical republicans at the time of the Revolution who favored a strong central government.

Above, the demolition of the Bastille in July 1789. Stones from the prison-fortress, which was stormed by a Paris mob, were sent as souvenirs to Revolutionaries throughout the country. Right, Camille Desmoulins, portrayed with his family. A powerful orator, Desmoulins was credited with inspiring the July revolt in Paris.

UNITE.
ET
INDIVISIBILITE
DE LA
RÉPUBLIQUE.
LIBERTÉ,
ÉGALITÉ,
FRATERNITÉ
OU LA MORT

CALENDRIER

AUTOMNE

HIVER

*Left, a placard with the motto of the Rev-
olution, the tricolor, and the liberty cap,
the cap worn by emancipated slaves in
ancient Roman times. Above, the Revolutionary Calendar. September 22, 1792,
the day the monarchy was abolished in
France, was declared the beginning of
"Year I of the Republic." Each month of
the new calendar year consisted of three
ten-day weeks.*

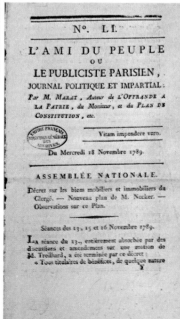

The call to revolution

The most effective weapon of the French Revolution was not the pike brandished by the sans-culotte but rather the printing press. With the summoning of the States-General in 1789—for the first time in over a hundred and fifty years—every electoral assembly in France was given the right to present a petition of grievances to the king. The opportunity inspired a flood of pamphlets, posters, and political essays. Newspapers, some written entirely by a single individual, were founded in Paris at the rate of one or two a week, and as many as one hundred pamphlets were issued each month. These writings ranged from the most strident and ephemeral propaganda to such influential essays as the Abbé Sieyès' *What is the Third Estate?* which argued forcefully that the nobility and the clergy were parasitic classes.

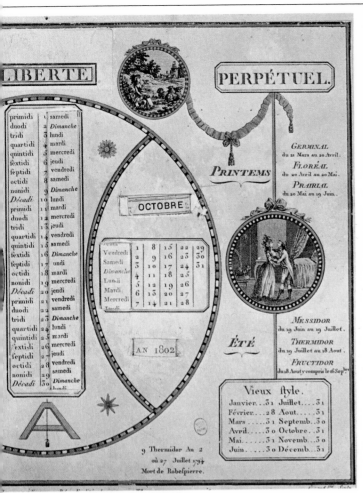

Near left, an identity card issued in 1792. Passes, identity documents, and ration cards helped stem the civil and economic disorders rife during the Revolution. Immediately below, the frontispiece of a Revolutionary calendar, which depicts the guillotined heads of condemned "enemies of the Revolution."

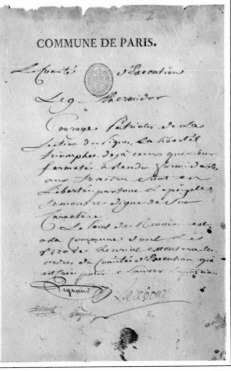

[Je]an Paul Marat's radical newspaper, L'Ami du [Pe]uple (left), called for vigilante attacks on po[liti]cal prisoners and a revolutionary dictatorship. [Ab]ove, a caricature depicting "the enemies of [Fr]ance." The British prime minister, William [Pit]t (on stilts), is shown leading the first anti-[Fr]ench coalition.

Right, a letter of encouragement from Robespierre to the Commune of Paris, the ruling body of Paris from 1792 to 1794. Urged on by Robespierre, local committees of Jacobin radicals had seized control of the municipal government and the National Guard. Many Commune members were executed after Robespierre's fall in 1794.

Above, the Marquis de Lafayette as commander of the National Guard. He is shown presiding over the Festival of the Federation, a Revolutionary holiday commemorating the storming of the Bastille. This pike-bearing woman (left) exemplifies the bold militant spirit of the sansculottes, the extreme republicans of the Revolution.

ignominious failure. In early June 1793, the Buona-partes were forced to flee to Toulon, and their home in Ajaccio was sacked by angry neighbors.

While Napoleon was sinking in the quagmire Corsican politics, the National Assembly was ener-getically pursuing "the regeneration of France" along the lines of a centralized constitutional monarchy. The ancient provinces were abolished and eighty-three "departments" created in their place, each sub-ordinate to the central government. Much of the Church's extensive property was seized to pay the kingdom's debts, and the Church itself was declared subject to state control.

The Revolutionary government's attempt to reor-ganize the French Catholic Church, together with the revival of France's military potential, brought the Revolution to its turning point. Many Catholics were offended by the Church's subordination to secular power, reactionaries were enraged by the destruction of ancient privileges, and many moderates and con-servatives were wary of the tendency of the revolu-tionary leaders to justify everything in the name of abstract principles. Louis XVI's fellow monarchs throughout Europe at first alternated between fasci-nation with French attempts to attain progressive ob-jectives and satisfaction at seeing France plunged into political turmoil. By 1790, however, they had come to fear that a successful revolution in France would both contaminate their own subjects with subversive ideas and upset the European balance of power.

Many Frenchmen believed that Louis XVI, per-ceiving growing foreign and internal resistance to the Revolution, had decided to intrigue with counter-revolutionaries and even encourage foreign powers to attack. In June 1791, his actions having aroused the suspicions of revolutionary leaders, Louis tried un-successfully to flee abroad. That autumn the National Assembly completed its labors by giving France a new constitution severely limiting royal power. A new parliamentary body—the Legislative Assembly—was elected soon after.

In the Legislative Assembly the increasingly influ-ential Girondist party openly advocated war against the hostile powers of Europe in the hope that a short victorious campaign would solidify patriotic support for the Revolution and extend France's borders. The powers played into the Girondists' hands by making what were interpreted as threats against the Revolu-tion. In April 1792 the Assembly declared war on Austria and Prussia.

At first, the war went badly for the French. Alarmed by news of defeats, the people of Paris were thrown into a frenzy by a manifesto issued in the name of the duke of Brunswick, the commander of

Left, the Festival of the Federation, held on Paris' Champ de Mars in July 1790 to mark the first anniversary of the fall of the Bastille. Below, a coin commemorating the festival. Above, the execution of Louis XVI on January 21, 1793.

the Austrian and Prussian forces, warning the French to guarantee the safety of the royal family or face "memorable vengeance." Far from cowering, the Parisians took to the streets in great numbers. A mob assaulted the Tuileries palace, the king's residence, and Louis was "suspended" as monarch. Other mobs massacred suspected counterrevolutionaries held in the city's prisons. On September 22, 1792, the monarchy was abolished and France declared a republic. Fatefully, the proclamation of the republic coincided with a dramatic turn of military fortunes, and by late 1792 French armies were advancing victoriously into Belgium and the Rhineland. In a mood of patriotic fervor and militant republicanism, Louis was tried for treason by the National Convention (which had taken the place of the Legislative Assembly), and on January 21, 1793, he was executed.

For the first time in the course of the Revolution the middle-class leadership pledged itself to the interests of the Parisian sans-culottes—the petty shopkeepers, artisans, and day laborers who were the driving force of the city's revolutionary mobs. In theory the new republican regime was far more democratic than any that had preceded it; in practice, however, it suspended the liberal constitution adopted in 1793

for the duration of the national emergency. The sit ation grew more critical in the summer of 1793, wh news came of defeats at the front and of royalist an tax and antidraft movements in the countryside.

The Girondists, who had precipitated the war, f from power, and the Convention came to be don nated by the radical middle-class Jacobin part Day-to-day administration was entrusted to t twelve-man Committee of Public Safety, whose m prominent member was Maximilien Robespier "the Incorruptible." A man of lofty, inflexible prin ples and hitherto an outspoken defender of fr speech and a free press, Robespierre arrived at t chilling conclusion that Revolutionary France cou survive only by supreme acts of republican virtu including the ruthless application of terror again those guilty of treason, corruption, and divisive part sanship. Wave after wave of persons convicted these crimes was sent to the guillotine: the form queen, "aristocrats," clergy, speculators, black ma keters, draft dodgers, thieves, prostitutes, provinci rebels, royalists, Girondists, and eventually Robe pierre's own Jacobin critics and rivals. Largely Robespierre's insistence, religious worship was abc ished in late 1793—patriots were henceforth to wo

...mong the privileges secured by ...e Revolutionaries was the ...ght to decapitation. This ...ethod of execution, instanta-...eous and carrying no stigma ...f dishonor, had previously ...en reserved for the nobility. ...octor Joseph Ignace Guillotin ...bove) suggested the idea for a ...achine (right) that would be ...ficient enough for general ...se—the guillotine.

...eft, The Roll Call of the Last ...ictims of the Terror *by ...harles Louis Muller. By 1794, ...evolutionary courts were em-...owered to convict all "enemies ...f the people." The victims in-...luded increasing numbers of ...iddle- and lower-class indi-...iduals accused of hoarding ...roperty or making antigovern-...ent remarks.*

The Bonaparte family

Like any good head of a Corsican family, Napoleon provided for his family—by parceling out conquered lands and assigning royal titles—and expected gratitude in return. He was destined, however, to be disappointed. Louis, whom Napoleon had once regarded as a potential heir, proved the most troublesome of the brothers and sisters. A hopeless hypochondriac who could not abide his wife, Hortense (the daughter of Napoleon's first wife, Joséphine), he angered Napoleon by siding with his Dutch subjects against the emperor's will. Brother Jérôme's Westphalian court attracted so many fortune-hunting actresses that it came to resemble a comic opera set, and his pleas on behalf of his overtaxed subjects brought down Napoleon's wrath. Many more family quarrels, large and small, were stirred up by Napoleon's own mother, who made no secret of her view that her son's success was a jest of fate.

Left, a view of the Ajaccio region of Corsica. Below, the dining room of the house in Ajaccio where Napoleon was born. Letizia Buonaparte (right), known as Madame Mère, was a formidable woman who never hesitated to defend her other children in their quarrels with her most famous son. She bore eleven children (three of whom did not survive infancy) by age thirty-three and outlived Napoleon, dying in 1836.

This page, seven portraits depicting Napoleon's brothers and sisters. Top row: Joseph, king of Naples and later of Spain; Louis, king of Holland until 1810. Second row: Lucien, exiled in 1810 for opposing Napoleon's policies; Jérôme, named king of Westphalia in 1807. Third row: Maria Anna Elisa, made grand duchess of Tuscany in 1809; Carolina, who married Joachim Murat and became queen of Naples. Left, Maria Paulina, a celebrated beauty, who married Prince Camillo Borghese.

When Frederick William II of Prussia (above) and Leopold II, the Holy Roman emperor (below), began planning for war against France at the time of the Revolution, they anticipated an easy victory. But Leopold died suddenly in March 1792, and by November the French Republic had won its first victory over the Austrians at Jemappes in Belgium (center right). At home, France was torn by rebellion. In August 1793 the British entered the Mediterranean port city of Toulon (above right) at the invitation of pro-Bourbon insurgents. A royalist rebellion also flared up in the western province of the Vendée (below right).

ip Reason, Virtue, and Innocence—and a new calendar was introduced that began with Year I of the epublic (September 22, 1792).

Robespierre and the other members of the Committee of Public Safety set about consolidating rench defense. In August 1793 the National Convention decreed a total mobilization. "Young men ill go to the front," the order read. "Married men ill transport foodstuffs; women will make tents and niforms and serve in the hospitals; children will tear gs into lint."

The very attempt to organize on this scale signaled new era in European warfare. Frenchmen, many of em from middle-class families who would never ave considered serving in the ranks under the former gime, marched off to the front singing "The Marillaise." These soldiers were eager to fight, imbued ith the conviction that they were defending their ation in a just cause. Unfortunately for the profesonal army units they joined, they were also unained, undisciplined, and not at all enthusiastic bout taking orders from aristocrats.

The task of welding elements of the old and new rmies into an effective fighting force fell to Lazare arnot, a former army engineer who had become a ember of the Committee of Public Safety. Carnot

reorganized transport and secured the munitions and supplies the army desperately needed. He also began recruiting military officers from nonnoble backgrounds to fill vacancies and assume commands from noble-born officers no longer considered politically reliable. Carnot, a commoner, had been unable to rise above the rank of captain in the pre-Revolutionary army, so this project was especially close to his heart.

Napoleon, technically from a noble family but middle class for all practical purposes, was just the sort of officer who was likely to rise in the reorganized army. His long absence in Corsica had almost lost him his standing as a regular officer, but in the summer of 1792 he had returned to Paris to claim reinstatement. There, coincidentally, he had witnessed the mob's invasion of the Tuileries in June, when Louis XVI was forced to don the revolutionaries' tri-

On July 27, 1794, Robespierre and his closest associates were denounced by the National Convention—the French assembly—and arrested (above).

Below, Jean Paul Marat, a journalist and revolutionary, who was assassinated in his bath by a young supporter of the conservative Girondin faction.

Near right, a sans-culotte, or extreme republican. Far right, Napoleon, a Jacobin supporter, imprisoned soon after the fall Robespierre.

color cockade. Contemptuous of the king and the mob alike, the young officer remarked that if he were king such a scene would never have occurred. But Napoleon's hunger for glory was already tempered by an appreciation of the realities of power, and he wrote to his brother Joseph of his determination to "keep on the right side of those who have been and can be my friends." His brother Lucien had nothing but distaste for this brand of pragmatism. "I believe," Lucien wrote, "that a man should place himself above circumstances. . . . The most hated men in history are those that sail according to the wind. . . . I have always discerned in Napoleon a purely selfish ambition that overrules his patriotism. I am convinced that he is a dangerous man in a free state. . . . I think that if he were a king he would certainly be a tyrant."

The summer after these prophetic lines were written the Buonapartes were expelled from Corsica, and Napoleon, now responsible for his mother and younger siblings, began to look toward his future in the

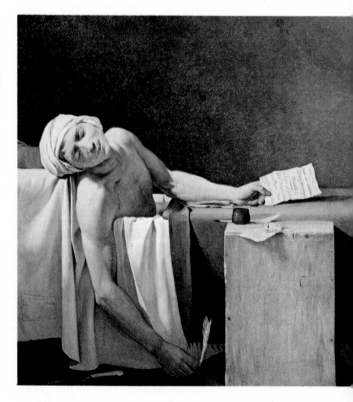

my of Carnot. His disillusionment with politics in Corsica was expressed in a pamphlet that supported the Parisian Jacobins and inveighed against federalist tendencies in the provinces. The pamphlet brought him a promotion to captain. By October he was presenting a plan for an artillery assault on Toulon, which royalist insurgents had surrendered to the British fleet. When Toulon fell, he emerged with the lion's share of the credit, prompting the remark by his commander that "even if his country were to be ungrateful to him, this officer would see to his own promotion." Indeed, Napoleon finished 1793 with the rank of brigadier general.

In July 1794, Robespierre was sent to the guillotine by Jacobins who feared that they were about to become the next victims of the Republic of Virtue. Napoleon, as a loyal supporter of Robespierre's brother Augustin in the Army of Italy, was briefly placed under house arrest, escaping a worse fate only through the intervention of Antoine Christophe Saliceti, a prominent fellow Corsican. Notwithstanding this close call, Napoleon felt confident enough to refuse the offer of an infantry command against the royalist peasants and nobles of the Vendée region in western France. Realizing that this politically risky assignment might jeopardize his career, Napoleon instead chose to take up residence in Paris and await new opportunities.

General Bonaparte—he soon began to use this more "French" spelling of his surname—found the mood in Paris much to his liking. With the coup against Robespierre, leadership of the Revolution returned to the more conservative middle-class element. Although rampant inflation and food shortages were driving the poor and the sans-culottes to desperation, the middle class believed it was once again politically correct to live the good life. Restaurants and theaters were crowded, and the salons of Madame de Staël and Madame Récamier were once again magnets for

...ft, the battle of Lodi, fought near Milan in ...ay 1796, at which Napoleon decisively de...ited the Austrians.

...apoleon was quick to use his victories in the ...ld as a springboard to political power. In ...'97, without official authority, he nego...ted the Peace of Leoben (below left), which ...ved the way for a Franco-Austrian settle...ent in Italy. The anti-Revolutionary stance ... Pope Pius VI (below) and the murder in ...me of Nicolas-Jean Hugou de Bassville, a ...ench diplomat (right, seen inside his car...age), provided pretexts for a French inva...n of the Eternal City in 1798.

...e influential and the would-be influential. As Na-...oleon wrote to his brother Joseph: "Here in Paris, ...xury, enjoyment and the arts are reassuming their ...d sway in surprising fashion.... Smart carriages ...nd fashionably dressed people are once more in the ...reets; they have the air of waking up after a long ...ream, and forgetting that they had ever ceased to ...isplay themselves."

Napoleon was still enjoying the theaters and boul-...vards when preparations for a plebiscite on a new ...onstitution and protests against high prices gave rise ...o a new wave of civil disorder. On October 5, 1795, ...olumns of royalist-inspired insurgents marched on ...e National Convention. Summoned to defend the ...overnment, Napoleon did not hesitate to disperse ...e lightly armed marchers with cannon fire—"a ...hiff of grapeshot," he later called it. The govern-...ent was saved, and the grateful National Conven-...on named Napoleon commander in chief of the ...rmy of the Interior.

The defeat of the rebels, whom Napoleon described

Ludovico Manin (immediately above), the last doge of Venice, surrendered to the French in the Doges' Palace (above left) in 1797.

as "the enemy," was not his only conquest in Paris. The next March he married Joséphine de Beauharnais, a Creole from the West Indian island of Martinique. Ornamental but not excessively virtuous, Joséphine embodied the very characteristics that Napoleon was wont to cite in justifying his contempt for the female sex. He nonetheless found her very alluring, and her connections with the salon society he had once dismissed as "effeminate" only added to her charms.

On March 11, Napoleon left for Italy to assume command of the French Army there. The Army of Italy had become the neglected stepchild of the French military effort. The main theater of the war was on the Rhine, where two French armies with about one hundred thousand men each appeared to

Above, Maria Paulina's two husbands, Prin[ce] Camillo Borghese (left) and General Char[les] Victor Emmanuel Leclerc (right). Left, Mar[ia] Paulina as Venus.

The imperial Venus

While Napoleon was subjugating Europe, his sister Maria Paulina engaged in the conquest of fashionable society. As a young woman, Maria Paulina had dutifully wed General Charles Victor Emmanuel Leclerc, one of Napoleon's favorite officers. But when Leclerc died of yellow fever in Haiti she chose a second husband for herself—Prince Camillo Borghese—and thus gained a title on her own initiative.

Maria Paulina relished her role as the reigning hostess of Paris. She entertained visitors while lounging in her milk bath and once, during a brief stay in Rome, posed nude for the Neoclassical sculptor Antonio Canova. (The princess insisted that Canova represent her as Venus.) Such activities infuriated Napoleon, and when one of Maria Paulina's lavish entertainments drew public criticism, he forced her to restage it for five hundred middle-class guests.

In the end, Maria Paulina proved to be the Bonaparte most loyal to Napoleon. She supported her brother's marriage to Marie Louise in 1810 and later followed him to his place of exile on the island of Elba, where her high-spirited parties created a cover for Napoleon's escape preparations.

Because Maria Paulina found the Borghese Palace in Rome (above) too dull, she set up her own household at the Villa Paolina (left), also in Rome. She owned another home in Paris and traveled frequently to European spas. When her husband had occasion to live under her roof, she billed him for food and lodgings.

A notorious spendthrift, Maria Paulina amassed a fabulous jewelry collection—and then tried to economize by saving on candles. This page from one of her account books (far left) dates from 1820, when she was forced to curtail the extravagant lifestyle that had earned her the nickname "Our Lady of the Frills." Near left, a mirror and snuffbox that belonged to Maria Paulina. Above, an aquarelle depicting the interior of the Villa Paolina.

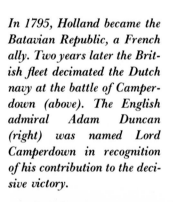

In 1795, Holland became the Batavian Republic, a French ally. Two years later the British fleet decimated the Dutch navy at the battle of Camperdown (above). The English admiral Adam Duncan (right) was named Lord Camperdown in recognition of his contribution to the decisive victory.

Despite Britain's overwhelmi[ng] naval supremacy, an attempt [to] land British troops in the B[a-] tavian Republic in 1799 (le[ft]) ended in a humiliating defe[at.] Although republican Fran[ce] had been able to introduce co[n-] scription, this was not possi[ble] in England. The British cons[e-] quently lacked the strength f[or] a large-scale invasion of t[he] Continent.

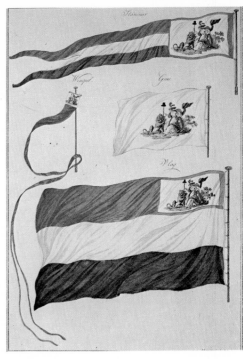

Left, a "secret army" for the invasion of England, assembled at the Dutch port of Vlissingen (Flushing) in 1799. Napoleon, fresh from his campaign in Egypt, was named to command the invasion but pronounced the plan too risky. Above, French naval pennants with depictions of the goddess of liberty.

ave a good chance of defeating the Austrians and then pushing on to the Hapsburg capital of Vienna. Nothing much was expected of the undermanned and demoralized force in Italy, but within a few short weeks Napoleon had led his men to a string of astounding victories. From the beginning, the new commander's fiery speeches and evident determination inspired troops who had seemed beyond inspiration. Even more important, Napoleon did not allow his army to wear itself out attacking the heavily fortified Austrian positions in the Alps. Marching with lightning speed, his army crossed the Po River, bypassed Milan, and defeated the Austrians at Lodi, twenty miles southeast of Milan, on May 10. At the end of his life, Napoleon was to look back to Lodi as the turning point in his career. "From that moment," he wrote, "I foresaw what I might be. Already I felt the earth flee from beneath me, as if I were being carried into the sky."

In the weeks that followed, the French swept through Italy, their progress aided by Napoleon's promise that he had come to free the peninsula from tyrants. The expectations of the Italian republicans were shattered when Napoleon signed armistices with the king of Sardinia and the pope. Entering Milan five days after the battle of Lodi, he demanded a reparation of twenty million French francs. As the army continued its southward march, art treasures were gathered up for transport to France. In the spring of 1797, Napoleon deliberately provoked an incident with neutral Venice and demanded a ransom that included ships, paintings by Titian and Tintoretto, five hundred manuscripts, and the ancient Roman bronze horses that had guarded the portals of St. Mark's Cathedral since they were seized from Constantinople in the thirteenth century.

The five-man Directory that governed France soon learned that the general enriching its treasury had no intention of meekly obeying orders. Having driven the Austrians back across the Alps, Napoleon acted on his own authority to negotiate an Italian settlement. Discussions with the Austrians, which culmi-

Napoleon and Italian unification

"I have always thought about rendering the Italian Nation free and independent." This statement by Napoleon, part of the very speech that announced the transformation of the Italian Republic into a kingdom in 1805, was intended to keep northern Italian liberals loyal to the emperor. In reality, the appointment of Eugène de Beauharnais as Napoleon's viceroy put an end to the fiction of Italian independence. Eugène made Italy perhaps the most stable and successful of the satellite kingdoms but could not stem the growth of nationalism. While a united national government was not in Napoleon's plans for the Italian peninsula, the emperor did much to create the expectations that made unification eventually possible.

Right, the palace of the Senate in Milan. Milan became capital of the Cisalpine Republic in 1797 and capital of the Kingdom of Italy in 1805.

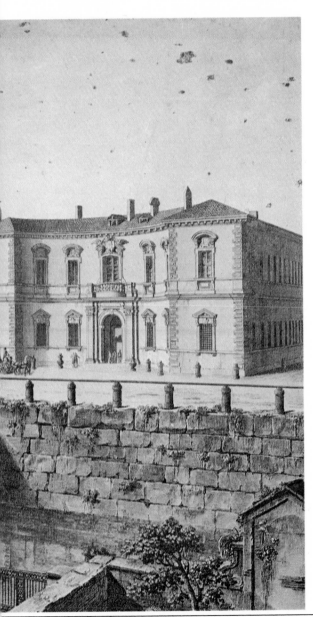

Above, uniforms of Italian soldiers in the Napoleonic period (left to right): a royal guard of the Naval Equipment Corps, an honor guard of the Milan Company, a sharpshooter, a horseman of the dragoon corps, and a member of the Fourth Light Infantry.

Above, the first Italian tricolor, adopted by the Lombardy Cavalry Legion in 1796. Left, an officer of the Cisalpine Republic. Below, a coin showing the Cisalpine Republic paying homage to France.

nated in the Treaty of Campo Formio, ceded to France the entire left bank of the Rhine—including some territory that was not Austria's to give. Italian patriots were pacified by the creation of the Cisalpine Republic in northern Italy, and Austria received the Venetian Republic.

Napoleon returned home to a hero's welcome in Paris. The French Republic had emerged from the war with its territory substantially enlarged, and pro-French republics had been established in Holland, Belgium, Switzerland, and Italy. Now, with the Austrians stymied, the French people could afford to savor their victory. To them, Napoleon combined the

Above left, Napoleon, the savior of his country, confront ing a legislature unwilling to be saved. This painting depicts Napoleon's appearance before the Council of Five Hundred, a chamber of the legislature, on 19 Brumaire of the Year VIII (November 10, 1799). Some of the Five Hundred denounced Napoleon as a dictator and were driven from the room by armed guards. The government formed after the coup of 18 Brumaire was a triumvirate but only Napoleon had real power. Others who served at one time or another as consuls were Charles François Lebrun (top), the Abbé Sieyès (center), and Jean Jacques Régis de Cambacérès (immediately above).

st qualities of citizen-soldier and statesman and itomized the hard-won international respectability the revolutionary regime.

Of France's enemies, only Britain remained a reat. Some in France urged an immediate invasion. eneral Bonaparte, appointed commander in chief of ance's Army of England, soon vetoed a plan for tting men and munitions across the Channel. As a ss risky alternative, he proposed an expedition ainst Egypt, a country that could act as a bulwark ainst the British in India. Technically a part of the ttoman Empire, Egypt was ruled by the warrior ste known as the Mamelukes, fierce but undisci- ined cavalrymen who practiced homosexuality and plenished their numbers with slaves purchased as ildren and trained in the martial arts. Napoleon asoned that the Mamelukes, a relic of the past, ould be easy prey for a disciplined modern force. In e meantime, Charles Maurice de Talleyrand- érigord, the French foreign minister, promised to nooth matters over with the Ottoman Turks and ep them out of the fray.

The French naval squadron sailed from Toulon in May 1798. Admiral Horatio Nelson, who was pursu- g the French with fourteen British ships, surmised

Napoleon's destination and headed for Alexandria. Having unwittingly passed the French squadron on the fogbound seas, he arrived to find the harbor empty. After two days there, convinced that the French had outsmarted him, Nelson left for Crete— only hours before the first of Napoleon's ships dropped anchor at Alexandria.

Napoleon's behavior as ruler of Egypt provided early evidence of the megalomania that was eventu- ally to destroy him. Issuing edicts in the name of "Sultan Bonaparte," Napoleon declared himself the champion of the Egyptian people and hinted that he and his entire army would soon embrace Islam. (The suggestion was received by the local inhabitants with the cynicism it merited.) Besides enhancing his own reputation, however, Napoleon contributed to the beginnings of Western-style civil government in

Below, a design for a sculpture by Pierre-Paul Prud'hon called **The Triumph of Consul Bo- naparte.** *Napoleon believed that art should be the handmaiden of politics and encouraged the production of grandiose Neo- classical monuments.*

Following pages, **The Battle of the Pyramids** *by F. Watteau de Lille. Typical of many paintings representing Napo- leon's exploits, it stretches the truth for heroic effect. The bat- tle was actually fought ten miles away from the pyramids.*

Left, the French army making its way through the Great St. Bernard Pass in the Alps in May 1800.

Above, Jacques Louis David's romanticized portrait of Napoleon leading his army through the Alps on a white charger.

gypt through his conquest and occupation. He also lvanced scholarship by including in his expedition-y force one hundred and fifty French scholars, hose work laid the basis for modern Egyptology.

Militarily, the Egyptian campaign was a fiasco. dmiral Nelson returned in August 1798 and soundly efeated the French in the battle of Abukir Bay. With pplies from France reduced to a mere trickle, Na-oleon's soldiers discovered that it was no easy matter live off the land in a desert country where even inking water was precious. Morever, Talleyrand's surance that the Ottoman Turks would stay out of e war proved to be false. With his army decimated plague and eye disease, Napoleon made a desper-e foray into Syria, hoping to cut off the Turkish lvance. Instead, the seaport fortress of Acre success-lly resisted the French siege.

With France shown to be less than invincible, reat Britain, Austria, Russia, and Turkey were em-oldened to form an anti-French coalition. The gov-nment in Paris was in turmoil, with three of the five irectors planning coups d'état. When Napoleon arned of these developments (through newspapers ocured from a British officer serving with the urks), he decided that the time had come for him to ave Egypt. On August 18, he and his entourage left Cairo and slipped through the British blockade. They left behind them a letter to General Jean Baptiste Kléber, the new commander in chief, informing him that the situation in Egypt was now his responsibility.

Throughout his Egyptian campaign, Napoleon had dispatched triumphal reports to France—whether or not they reflected actual performance on the bat-tlefield. These communiqués had done their work, and Napoleon was welcomed as a hero on his return to Paris. He found two of the five members of the Directory, Pierre Roger Ducos and the Abbé Sieyès (the latter had been the Third Estate's most eloquent spokesman in 1789), well along in their own plans to overthrow the government. The general was brought into the plot mostly as a figurehead, but gradually he assumed the dominant role. On 18 Brumaire of the Year VIII (November 9, 1799), the coup d'état was successfully carried out.

Despite the considerable bungling that attended the coup of 18 Brumaire, the new regime was wel-comed by a middle class eager for stability and peace. To the loud applause of respectable opinion, Napo-leon issued a proclamation that declared: "Citizens, the Revolution is stabilized on the principles on which it began. The Revolution is over."

The battle of Marengo (left), fought in northwestern Italy in June 1800, was one of Napoleon's most celebrated victories. The battle's fame was a testament to Napoleon's talent for self-aggrandizement: The true hero, General Louis Charles Antoine Desaix de Veygoux (shown falling from his horse in the center left of this painting), was relegated to a supporting role in reports of the fighting against the Austrians. Napoleon can be seen on his horse not far below Desaix de Veygoux, set off against a light smoke cloud. Above, the Marengo plain today.

The Code Napoléon

The civil code of 1804, later known as the Code Napoléon, was destined to be the Napoleonic Empire's most enduring legacy. Even judged by the standards of the time, the code was by no means an ideal document, sacrificing, for example, the interests of labor and women to the goal of protecting property rights. Nevertheless, the code's 2,281 articles were recognized everywhere as a concise statement of the rights won by the French Revolution. The Code Napoléon became the model for legal codes throughout the world, not only in the countries that had been part of Napoleon's empire but in Louisiana, Latin America, Asia, and Africa.

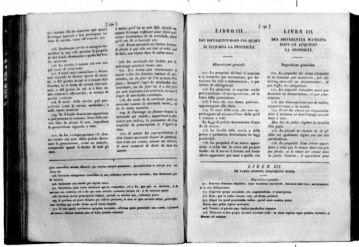

The new constitution proclaimed on December 1 1799, made Napoleon Bonaparte First Consul; co suls Ducos and Sieyès were relegated to supportir roles. Universal suffrage was granted, but the vo had little practical significance. Aside from plet scites—which always resulted in overwhelming m jorities for the First Consul, since the votes were pu licly recorded in front of election officials—there w to be a system of indirect elections to choose "not bles" eligible for appointment to legislative bodie later, this provision was diluted still further. The re legislative power was exercised by the First Cons through his council of state. As the Abbé Sieyès d scribed it, the principle of the new constitution w "authority from above; consent from below."

The years after Napoleon's elevation to First Co sul saw sweeping reforms in France's legal, admini

Left, Italian patriots meeting at Lyon in 1802 to proclaim the Republic of Italy. Napoleon (seated on the dais) was named the republic's president. Below, the crown used at Napoleon's coronation as king of Italy in 1805.

Above, Pope Pius VII receiving the text of the Concordat of 1801 (between France and the papacy) from Cardinal Ercole Consalvi. The agreement ended the rift between church and state produced by some of the Revolution's reforms.

ative, and educational structures. In education, for ample, the First Consul continued the trend toward cularization. Napoleon, who had little interest in e goal of universal primary education, concentrated establishing *lycées,* or state-supported secondary hools. Within a few years, teachers became public ployees, not only in the lycées but also in privately pported schools. The benefits of the new system, ich included a large number of government schol- ships, went primarily to the sons of military officers d the middle class. Women did not figure in Napo- n's educational reforms at all—he was convinced at any learning beyond home tutoring or a few ars in a convent school could only serve to corrupt e female character.

Napoleon had no objection to pacifying conserva- es by repairing the breach between the Roman

Catholic Church and the Revolutionary French state, which had culminated in the widespread public wor- ship of Reason in 1793. Napoleon's terms for the set- tlement—the Vatican's sanction of the confiscation of Church property, its recognition of the First Consul's right to appoint all French bishops, and its agreement that parish priests be salaried state officials—were ac- cepted by Pope Pius VII in the Concordat of 1801. (In weighing the alternatives, the pope was well aware that Napoleon had the means to drive him from Rome.) Later, French Protestant churches came under comparable regulations, and Jewish leaders were asked to approve assimilationist laws permitting divorce and rendering Jews subject to military service.

France under Napoleon's regime was given a strongly centralized administrative system, the most important functionaries of which were the appointed prefects and subprefects of each locality. The police were reorganized into a national system, though Napoleon was careful not to concentrate too much power in the hands of Joseph Fouché, his able and independent-minded minister of police—and a former Jacobin terrorist. Such administrative changes were very much in the spirit of the Committee of Public Safety, which had constantly battled against the resistance of provincial forces. In the minds of many Frenchmen loyal to the Revolution, elected local governments were associated with reactionary obstruction and even royalism. Thus, bureaucratic centralization, which in practice augmented Napoleon's dictatorial power, was widely supported as a progressive measure, and the First Consul's administrative appointees were often recruited from among opportunistic ex-Jacobins.

Of course, the war remained the ultimate determinant of the success or failure of Napoleon's government. The French general André Masséna was besieged by the Austrians in Genoa, yet Napoleon was reluctant to concede any of France's power in Italy lest he forfeit his popular image as a leader untarnished by defeat. Impatient with the conservative strategies of General Jean Victor Moreau, who commanded the Army of the Rhine, Napoleon personally led the makeshift Army of Reserve on a daring crossing of the Great St. Bernard Pass in the Alps. Characteristically, Napoleon planned to move his troops quickly and engage the Austrians in a decisive battle that would cut off their path of retreat. The gamble almost led to disaster, for on June 14 the Austrians surprised Napoleon's divided and unprepared army near the village of Marengo in northwestern Italy. Except for the timely arrival of reinforcements under General Louis Charles Antoine Desaix de Veygoux, the battle of Marengo would have been an Austrian victory. Fortunately for the Napoleonic legend, Desaix was killed in the fighting and was remembered in battle reports as a loyal subordinate who died with the First Consul's name on his lips.

Austria's ability to wage war was destroyed by General Moreau's subsequent victories in Germany, which led to the Treaty of Lunéville in 1801. By terms of the agreement, France's control of the left bank of the Rhine was confirmed, the Cisalpine Republic of northern Italy was resurrected as a French ally, and Genoa and Piedmont became French dependencies. A year later, the war-weary British signed the Treaty of Amiens.

In the meantime, Napoleon was moving to eliminate his political opponents. He, like the Jacobins, had never believed in the principle of a loyal opposi-

Left, Napoleon I on the Imperial Throne *by Jean Auguste Dominique Ingres. The emperor wears royal ermine, the laurel crown of a Caesar, and a robe decorated with golden bees, his family symbol. The bedrooms of Napoleon (above) and Joséphine (below) at the chateau of Malmaison display the straight lines and classical proportions of the French Empire style. In place of the Rococo decoration associated with the pre-Revolutionary regime, artists turned to Classical motifs to express opulence and dignity. Right, the empress Joséphine.*

tion. Rousseau's idea of a "general will" that must necessarily triumph (a concept that had earlier appealed to Robespierre) was more to his liking. To Napoleon this meant that the government must mold public opinion as well as execute it. Already, in January 1800, he had ordered the closing of sixty of France's seventy-three newspapers. Unofficial but vigilant censorship became the rule. If the constitution stood in the way, it was either changed or ignored. As the First Consul said in 1801: "Every day brings the necessity to violate constitutional laws; it is the only way, otherwise progress would be impossible." Jacobin leaders who failed to give evidence of their loyalty were executed or exiled, and royalist insurgents in the provinces were ruthlessly suppressed.

In the spring of 1802, when the Treaty of Amiens went to the Senate for ratification, Napoleon suggested that the senators might want to confer on him some token honor in recognition of the "nation's gratitude." The Senate responded by voting to extend his term as consul for ten years. This was not what the First Consul had in mind, and he proposed that the matter be submitted to the people as a plebiscite. By the time the resolutions for the plebiscite had been framed, they called for Napoleon to become Consul for Life. The life consulship was duly approved by the people, who were given neither a positive alternative nor the chance to cast their ballots in secret. A provision allowing Napoleon to name his own successor was incorporated in a new constitution, one that gave Napoleon virtually monarchical powers.

*op, the battle of Trafalgar in October 1805. Although
ritain had been seized by war fever for two years, it was
prepared to mount an invasion of the Continent. Tra-
lgar gave the country a victory to celebrate at long last.
mediately above, Admiral Nelson, felled by an enemy
iper, lying mortally wounded on the deck of his flag-
ip, the* Victory. *Above right, the prow of the* Victory,
display at Portsmouth, England.*

Although many of Napoleon's oldest supporters,
including Fouché, were disturbed by his increasingly
dictatorial proclivities, the mood of France during the
months after the Treaty of Amiens was ebullient.
Paris was jammed with British tourists taking advantage of the first opportunity to visit the city in nine
years. Émigrés returned by the thousands, and finan-
ciers and speculators—however much Napoleon may
have distrusted them—prospered because of reforms
in the banking system and the currency. Young men
of more modest middle-class backgrounds found secure careers as bureaucrats and petty functionaries,
and living standards rose steadily. Although there

129

Top, the seizure of the German city of Ulm in October 1805. Immediately above, the French being welcomed in Munich. Below, the Napoleonic army entering Vienna on November 13, 1805.

was little personal freedom, many Frenchmen considered this a small price to pay for stability, prosperity, and peace. Even British visitors were impressed by French efficiency, and many argued that greater freedom of worship and equality of opportunity were to be found on the French side of the Channel.

The new civil code (later known as the Code Napoléon), adopted in 1804, gave enduring legal sanction to the changes that French society had undergone since 1789. Many of the significant rights won during the Revolution—equality of individuals before the law, the abolition of serfdom and feudal privileges, the right of commoners to acquire and amass private property—were now incorporated into the law. A few of the more advanced principles espoused by the Committee of Public Safety were abandoned, however, including recognition of the rights of labor.

Napoleon did not actually write the civil code; work on it had begun long before his rise to power, but he presided over many of the sessions in which proposed laws were discussed. Often he supported the most conservative alterations. In the new code, the father assumed the role of dictator within the family, able to control his wife's property and even to imprison recalcitrant children for up to six months. Illegitimacy once more became grounds for depriving a child of the right to inherit equally. Although Napoleon owed his rise to the propertied middle class and the individual rights it had secured under the Revolution, he remained suspicious of individualism and used the code to help shore up traditional institutions like the family.

The Consul for Life enjoyed the prerogatives of a king. Having moved to the Tuileries palace, Napoleon surrounded himself with liveried servants, reintroduced court etiquette, and chose four women from the old aristocracy to serve Joséphine as ladies in waiting. However, neither Napoleon's character nor public opinion would have permitted the profligacy of the pre-Revolutionary regime, so the court maintained a façade of propriety. Napoleon had become the world's first bourgeois monarch.

For another man this uncrowned kingship might have been enough, but Napoleon's faith in his "destiny" had by now grown too great for him to be satisfied with the title of Consul for Life—or with France alone. Napoleon desired a resumption of war, and this was easily arranged. Britain, which had grudgingly accepted the Treaty of Amiens, watched nervously as France adopted policies that seemed to threaten British commercial and colonial supremacy, imposing protective tariffs in France, acquiring the

Left, Napoleon and Holy Roman Emperor Francis II meeting after the French victory at Austerlitz in December 1805. Immediately below, Austerlitz at 10 A.M. by Simeon Fort. Napoleon had duped the allied Russian and Austrian forces into believing that the French army was in retreat; when the morning mist cleared, the Allies looked down from their position on Pratzen Plateau at the massed might of the French. Austerlitz at 4 P.M. (bottom) shows the French command surveying the last stages of the battle.

Napoleon in caricature

Napoleonic war was ideological war. Although the conflict was not simply a struggle between the sons of the Revolution and their aristocratic enemies, this was indeed how it appeared to many at the time. In some countries, notably Ireland, Napoleon became a popular hero, celebrated in ballads and folklore. Elsewhere he was the subject of vicious caricatures that portrayed him as an upstart commoner and the heir of the bloodthirsty Paris mob, whose excesses had been magnified many times over in the minds of the upper classes. To the English, he was "Boney," a boogieman figure whose name struck terror into the hearts of children. As one English nursery verse warned:

Baby, baby, he's a giant.
Tall and black as Rouen steeple,
And he dines and sups, rely on't,
Every day on naughty people.

Above, a Spanish cartoon entitled "Le Grand Empereur–Le Grand Operateur" (The Great Emperor–The Great Surgeon)—an allusion to the human costs of Napoleon's campaigns. The exact content and significance of this drawing are difficult to determine. According to one interpretation, Napoleon is represented here as a grizzled old man carrying a youthful mask, imperial trappings, and a satchel of magic healing powder—a useless powder, since he himself cannot be healed by it.

Below, "Napoleon Bonaparte Mummified." This Italian caricature refers to the entrapment of the French expeditionary force in Egypt after the battle of Abukir Bay in August 1798. Shortly after the French defeat, Napoleon turned over command of the French forces in Egypt to General Jean Baptiste Kléber and made his way to a Paris rife with antigovernment plots.

"The Imperial Skipper" (above) is a French cartoon from the time of Napoleon's last campaign. Napoleon, caught between the Prussian general Gebhard Leberecht von Blücher and the British duke of Wellington, is forced to "skip to their tune." "Sir," Napoleon says irritably to his oppressor Blücher, "this game displeases me. It my last turn."

Top, the imperial eagle carrying Napoleon to exile on Elba. "Murat Reviewing the Grande Armée" (immediately above) is an English caricature ridiculing the heterogeneity of the Napoleonic army. This German caricature of Napoleon (left) shows the emperor's face made up of corpses. Below, Napoleon occupying his new throne on Elba.

...low, Czar Alexander peer-...g through his spyglass at ...poleon, who has been cut ...wn to size by the Russian ...mpaign of 1812. The ...ench rout thrust Alexander ...o the heroic role he had ...vently desired.

1800 SECOND ITALIAN CAMPAIGN

Gran St. Bernard • Milan • Treviso
KINGDOM OF • VENETO • Verona
Turin LOMBARDY
Ticino Adige
Po
Marengo Po
SARDINIA
Genoa

1805 THIRD COALITION

CONFEDERATION
Rhine Elbe
FRANCE OF THE RHINE Prague
Strasbourg Elchingen Brno Austerlitz
Ulm AUSTRIAN EMPIRE
Munich Danube
Rhine Vienna Pressburg
SWISS Inn
CONFEDERATION

Napoleon and his empire

Napoleon, the quintessential man of action, reshaped Europe in less than two decades. Early campaigns in Italy and Egypt won the Corsican a hero's reputation in France. Participant in a coup d'état, "the Little Corporal" emerged as First Consul of France in 1799. In 1804 he crowned himself emperor.

The extensive Napoleonic Empire was in time brought down by a combination of anti-French coalitions and tactical blunders on Napoleon's part. His final defeat at Waterloo in 1815 marked the end of an era. France, stripped of its post-Revolutionary acquisitions, was never again the dominant power in Europe.

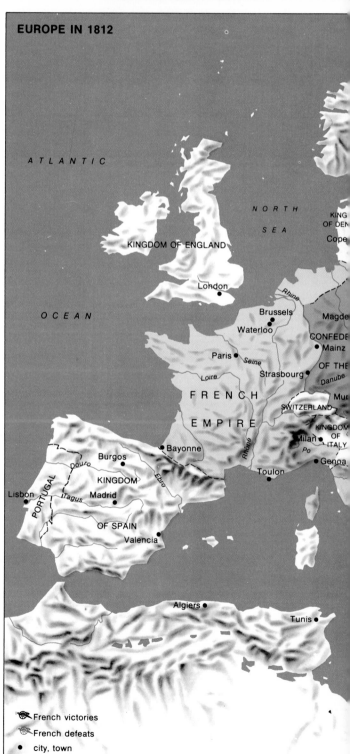

EUROPE IN 1812

ATLANTIC OCEAN
NORTH SEA
KING OF DEN
KINGDOM OF ENGLAND
Cope
London Rhine
Brussels Magde
Waterloo CONFE
Paris Seine Mainz
Loire Strasbourg OF THE
FRENCH Danube
Bayonne SWITZERLAND Mur
EMPIRE Rhone KINGDOM OF ITALY
Burgos Milan Po
Lisbon Douro KINGDOM Ebro Toulon Genoa
PORTUGAL Tagus Madrid
OF SPAIN
Valencia
Algiers Tunis

1798 EGYPTIAN CAMPAIGN

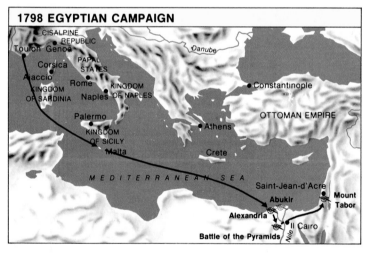

CISALPINE REPUBLIC
Toulon Genoa Danube
Corsica PAPAL STATES
Ajaccio Rome
KINGDOM Naples KINGDOM OF NAPLES Constantinople
OF SARDINIA
Palermo OTTOMAN EMPIRE
KINGDOM OF SICILY
Malta Athens Crete
MEDITERRANEAN SEA
Saint-Jean-d'Acre
Abukir Mount Tabor
Alexandria
Il Cairo
Battle of the Pyramids Nile

1796–1797 FIRST ITALIAN CAMPAIGN

Neumarkt
Tarvisio
Campo Formio Udine
REPUBLIC
LOMBARDY Rivoli Bassano
Milan Castiglione delle Stiviere Verona
Lodi Arcole OF VENICE
Po Ticino Mantua Adige
Turin Piacenza
OF SARDINIA Po
Cherasco
Dego Cairo Genoa
Millesimo Montenotte
Mondovi Carbona
Nice

🐢 French victories
🐢 French defeats
• city, town

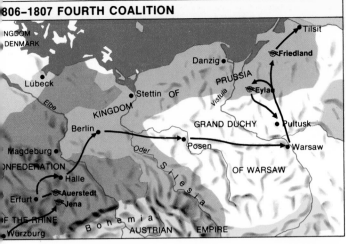

806–1807 FOURTH COALITION

KINGDOM OF DENMARK
Lübeck
Danzig
Stettin OF
PRUSSIA
Tilsit
Friedland
Berlin
Vistula
Eylau
Pultusk
Magdeburg
Oder
GRAND DUCHY
Posen
Warsaw
CONFEDERATION
Halle
OF WARSAW
Erfurt
Auerstedt
Jena
Silesia
Würzburg
OF THE RHINE
Bohemia
AUSTRIAN EMPIRE

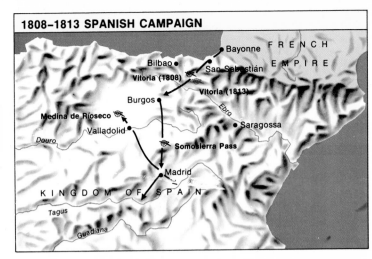

1808–1813 SPANISH CAMPAIGN

FRENCH EMPIRE
Bayonne
Bilbao
San Sebastián
Vitoria (1808)
Vitoria (1813)
Burgos
Ebro
Medina de Ríoseco
Saragossa
Douro
Valladolid
Somosierra Pass
Madrid
KINGDOM OF SPAIN
Tagus
Guadiana

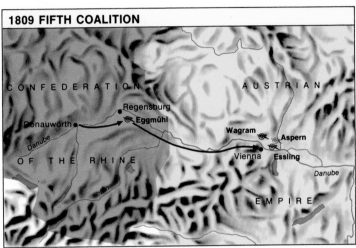

1809 FIFTH COALITION

CONFEDERATION
AUSTRIAN
Regensburg
Donauwörth
Eggmühl
Wagram
Aspern
Danube
Vienna
Essling
OF THE RHINE
Danube
EMPIRE

Stockholm
Volga
Moscow
Tilsit
Königsberg
PRUSSIA
Smolensk
Eylau
GRAND DUCHY
RUSSIAN EMPIRE
OF WARSAW
Warsaw
Vistula
Austerlitz
Don
USTRIAN
Kiev
Kharkov
Dnieper
Buda Pest
EMPIRE
Belgrade
Danube
Nikopol
BLACK SEA
Sofia
OTTOMAN
Constantinople
EMPIRE
Smyrna
Athens
MEDITERRANEAN SEA
Alexandria
Il Cairo
Nilo

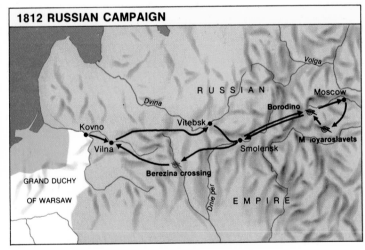

1812 RUSSIAN CAMPAIGN

RUSSIAN
Dvina
Moscow
Borodino
Kovno
Vitebsk
Vilna
Smolensk
M ioyaroslavets
Berezina crossing
GRAND DUCHY
Dnieper
OF WARSAW
EMPIRE

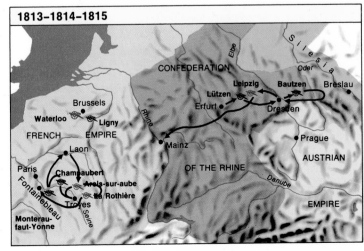

1813–1814–1815

CONFEDERATION
Elbe
Oder
Silesia
Leipzig
Bautzen
Breslau
Lützen
Erfurt
Dresden
Brussels
Rhine
Waterloo
Ligny
Mainz
Prague
FRENCH
EMPIRE
AUSTRIAN
Laon
Paris
Champaubert
OF THE RHINE
Fontainebleau
Arcis-sur-aube
Danube
la Rothière
EMPIRE
Troyes
Seine
Montereau-faut-Yonne

The battle of Jena (left), foug in October 1806, was ce brated as the engagement which Napoleon destroyed t fabled Prussian army; act ally, the crucial fighting too place at nearby Auerste Below left, the triumph French entry into Stettin (no Szczecin, in present-day P land) on October 31, 1806.

Louisiana Territory in America from Spain, and dispatching a French expedition to regain the West Indian island of Hispaniola from its liberator, the ex-slave Toussaint L'Ouverture. On the Continent, meanwhile, the French were continually intervening in the affairs of Holland and Switzerland (the Batavian and Helvetian republics). In addition, Napoleon appeared to regard Italy as his private country estate, and in 1802 he pressured the Italian Republic (for-

merly the Cisalpine Republic) into naming him i president.

Nor were the provocations unilateral. Britain ha second thoughts about evacuating Malta as agree upon in the Treaty of Amiens. In 1803, after Napo leon publicly berated the British ambassador for v olating one of the pact's key provisions, the Britis fleet seized French merchant ships on the high sea This was tantamount to a declaration of war.

low, Napoleon at the Battle of Eylau. *is bloody battle (fought in February '07), though counted as a French victory, ve rise to speculation that Napoleon had erplayed his hand in Prussia. After a more ccessful campaign during the summer, poleon met Czar Alexander and negotiated e Treaties of Tilsit on a barge in the Neman ver. Right, Napoleon and Alexander, with e czar's Cossack and Kalmuck guards de- cted at the right of the painting.*

Talleyrand had warned the British that "the first annon shot could bring into being a Gallic Empire." s it happened, Napoleon did not even wait for the utbreak of hostilities, using the uncovering of a roy- list plot as an excuse to assume the imperial title he raved. The plot, which included General Moreau, as exposed through the cunning of Fouché. The onspirators had supposedly been in contact with a ysterious "prince" who was prepared to enter France and assume the throne after Napoleon's fall. Napoleon was certain that this prince was the duke of Enghien, the son of a former émigré leader and resi- dent of the neutral duchy of Baden (in present-day West Germany). The duke had apparently been making surreptitious trips to the French city of Stras- bourg to visit his mistress, but he knew nothing of the plot. Nevertheless, Napoleon had him kidnaped in Baden, spirited into France, and summarily shot. The

The private life of a soldier-emperor

Napoleon's attitude toward luxury was shaped by his youthful experiences as a poor student in competition with the sons of the upper classes. As an adult, he appreciated wealth as a status symbol but only gradually learned to enjoy it. He began to accumulate a private fortune during the booty-rich Italian campaign of 1796 and soon after established a befittingly splendid household for himself and Joséphine at his chateau of Malmaison, west of Paris.

Having little use for social niceties, Napoleon retained the rough—sometimes bullying—manners of a soldier. He enjoyed opera and an occasional hunting party and became increasingly fond of expensively tailored clothes and ostentatious surroundings. Even during the French retreat from Moscow, the emperor was provided with a well-set table and his favorite wine.

These pages, views of the Grand Trianon at Versailles, where the emperor resided for a time after his divorce from Joséphine in 1809. Napoleon's bathroom (above) still contains his collection of colognes and reducing medicines. His bedroom (this page, below right) is filled with precious objects, including a Sèvres china clock. Near right, a portrait of Madame Récamier, a celebrated hostess and wit.

Above, the Grand Trianon. Below, a portrait of Marie Walewska, the Polish countess who was one of Napoleon's mistresses. Above right, Napoleon's chess set. Below right, the emperor's desk, with papers written in his own hand.

duke of Enghien's murder did a great deal to kindle memories of the Revolution in the minds of aristocrats throughout Europe .

Napoleon exploited this plot against his life by calling for a hereditary succession law and planning his own coronation as emperor. He had a statue of himself—dressed in the toga of a Roman emperor—erected in Paris' Place Vendôme, and a sword, said to have belonged to Charlemagne, was brought from the city of Aix-la-Chapelle (Aachen, now in West Germany) for use in the coronation ceremony. The cathedral of Notre Dame was so transformed in preparation for the grand event that, in the words of one

Parisian, "God himself would not have recogniz[ed] it."

Napoleon used the occasion of his approachi[ng] coronation to create the beginnings of an imperi[al] nobility. The Legion of Honor, intended as an awa[rd] for merit, now came to resemble the knightly orde[r] of pre-Revolutionary France. Napoleon's relativ[es] and closest associates received titles. Within a fe[w] years Napoleon was creating hereditary king[s,] princes, and dukes—among them associates who ha[d] fought for the abolition of the old aristocracy. A ne[w] imperial standard, combining the Revolution's tr[i]color, the Roman eagle, and the golden bees of th[e]

The rivalry between the Spanish king's he[ir] apparent, Prince Ferdinand of Asturi[as] (above), and the king's chief minister, M[a]nuel de Godoy (below), gave Napoleon t[he] opportunity to place Joseph Bonaparte on t[he] throne of Spain in 1808. French forces e[n]gaged in a difficult and bloody struggle f[or] control of Spain. Left, The French Cr[oss] the Sierra de Guadarrama. Above rig[ht,] two French views of Napoleon's entry i[n] Madrid in December 1808. Below right, T[he] Third of May 1808: The Execution of t[he] Defenders of Madrid by the Span[ish] painter Francisco Goya.

napartes, superseded the old royal fleur-de-lis. Finally, to ensure that the approaching coronation ould be suitably received, censorship of the press id the arts was redoubled.

The coronation took place on December 2, 1804. ope Pius VII, who had been persuaded to officiate, as upstaged at the crucial moment by Napoleon, ho took the crown from the pope's hands and placed on his own head—a gesture supposedly originated Charlemagne himself. The common people of aris, who were excluded from the ceremony, reacted the festivities with wary amusement. Royalists denounced the coronation as a farce, while Napoleon's

former colleagues from the officer corps of the republic were shocked. The monarchs of Europe viewed Napoleon's presumption as a threat to themselves, and liberal patriots, who had hailed Napoleon as the apostle of liberty, equality, and fraternity, came to see their hero in a new light. Beethoven, who had composed the *Eroica* Symphony with Napoleon in mind, hastily removed the emperor's name from the dedication. Italian nationalists were incensed when the Italian Republic was transformed into a kingdom, with Napoleon arriving in Milan in 1805 to celebrate a second triumphal coronation, this time as "King of All Italy."

The Grande Armée

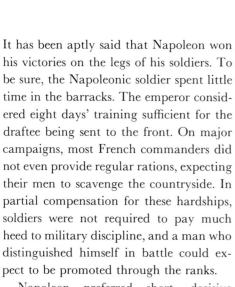

It has been aptly said that Napoleon won his victories on the legs of his soldiers. To be sure, the Napoleonic soldier spent little time in the barracks. The emperor considered eight days' training sufficient for the draftee being sent to the front. On major campaigns, most French commanders did not even provide regular rations, expecting their men to scavenge the countryside. In partial compensation for these hardships, soldiers were not required to pay much heed to military discipline, and a man who distinguished himself in battle could expect to be promoted through the ranks.

Napoleon preferred short, decisive wars—largely because he could not afford to fight long ones. His huge armies were always in need of arms and supplies, and the soldiers knew that they had to win quickly to survive. As long as Napoleon was victorious, esprit de corps was high, and the figure of the emperor inspired the steadfast loyalty of his troops.

Above far left, the golden eagle, prestigious symbol of the infantry divisions of the Grande Armée. Immediately above, a review of Napoleonic troops in 1814. Above right, three of Napoleon's generals: André Masséna (top), duke of Rivoli, who led the imperial army in Spain; Charles Pichegru (center), who was executed for plotting against Napoleon in 1803; and Jean Baptiste Kléber (below), who succeeded Napoleon as commander of French forces in Egypt.

These pages, below, Napoleonic troops (left to right): a lancer of the Imperial Guard, a hussar, a grenadier from a Swiss regiment, and an Egyptian soldier.

While Napoleon was occupied with founding an empire, the conflict with Britain grew more heated. The superior British fleet was wreaking havoc with French shipping, the French expedition to Hispaniola was foundering, and the British had occupied a number of small French and Dutch colonies in the Caribbean. Rather than risk losing the indefensible Louisiana Territory, Napoleon sold it to the United States in 1803 for a sum that did little more than cover French debts to that nation.

On the Continent, Britain was encountering resistance in its search for allies in another anti-French coalition. The Austrians were weary of war and Prus-sia was indecisive, hoping to side with whichev power would offer it Hanover, a possession of the ki of England that had been occupied by the Frenc

In 1803, Napoleon began massing troops at t port of Boulogne on the English Channel for a pr jected invasion of Britain. Fully aware of the diffic ties of ferrying troops across the well-defended stra by flatboats and barges, Napoleon had conceived t idea of sending French and Spanish ships to the We Indies, where they could lure a British squadron in battle and defeat it. With Franco-Spanish and Briti forces thus made roughly equal, the French ar Spanish ships were to hurry back to the Engli

Above, Gripsholm Castle, a residence of the Swedish royal family until the nineteenth century. Jean Baptiste Jules Bernadotte of France (right) was chosen by the childless King Charles XIII (below) to become the heir to the throne of Sweden. The Swedes were said to have been impressed by Bernadotte's military bearing and his chivalrous treatment of defeated enemies—and they also knew that Bernadotte was married to Désirée Clary, a childhood sweetheart of Napoleon and the sister-in-law of Joseph Bonaparte. Because of this family connection, Bernadotte managed to win Napoleon's approval for his new post in Sweden.

Bernadotte and Sweden

In 1807, Sweden and Swedish-held Fi land became pawns in the Franco-Russia Treaties of Tilsit, and the Swedish Crow was faced with a grave crisis. King Gu tavus IV, unable to reconcile himself to tl Russian occupation of Finland, was d posed two years later in favor of his elder and childless uncle, who was willing make peace. Hoping to placate Napoleo the new king offered to name the Frenc general Jean Baptiste Jules Bernadotte his successor.

Elected heir to the throne in 1810, Be nadotte subsequently gave notice that intended to defend Swedish interests. 1812 he refused to support Napoleon's i vasion of Russia, and a year later he joine the anti-French allies. In 1818, Bernadott became king as Charles XIV John founder of the royal line that reigns Sweden to this day.

annel and attempt to hold those waters long ough for the French troops to make their way safely English shores. The plan would have been a brilnt one if France had possessed a navy capable of ecuting it. As it was, the returning French and anish vessels got no farther than Spain, where in id-August of 1805 they were trapped inside Cádiz rbor by a British blockade. On October 21, 1805, poleon's fleet was all but annihilated off Spain's ape Trafalgar by British forces commanded by Adiral Nelson.

A few months earlier, Czar Alexander I of Russia d finally made up his mind to ally himself with

Britain. Alexander's decision to oppose Napoleon became the catalyst which led to the formation of an anti-French coalition that included Austria, Sweden, Naples, Britain, and Russia. Napoleon, for his part, had won the support of Bavaria and the other south German states (which saw a chance to break free from Austrian domination) and wasted no time in opening up a land campaign on the Continent. By October 15 the French army assembled at Ulm on the Danube, where it destroyed a major corps of the Austrian army. Advancing through Vienna, the French encountered the main body of Austrian and Russian troops near Austerlitz, a town in what is now Czech-

ove, Napoleon's principal adversaries (left right): Francis II, who was the last Holy man emperor; Czar Alexander of Russia, o became Napoleon's implacable foe after 12 and led the coalition that defeated ance in 1814; George, the Prince of Wales, o acted as regent of England after his faer, George III, was declared insane in 11; and Frederick William III of Prussia, o was goaded into opposing Napoleon by queen and public opinion.

Below, snuffboxes bearing the monograms and coats of arms of the emperors allied against France (left to right): Frederick William III, Francis II, and Alexander.

oslovakia. His forces outnumbered, Napoleon managed to trick the enemy into deploying its troops along a broad front and then cut its lines in half.

Austerlitz was a humiliating defeat for Czar Alexander, who had personally approved the tactics that led the Allied army into Napoleon's trap. The heaviest blow, however, fell on Austria, which had to withdraw from the war altogether and to surrender all claims in Italy. By the next summer, Napoleon w able to organize sixteen German states, led by B varia and Württemberg, into the puppet Confeder tion of the Rhine. This move formally abolished t. moribund Holy Roman Empire.

Now that Napoleon was master of western Europ Prussia belatedly decided to take up arms against t French. The army of the Prussians, though legenda

This page, scenes from campaign of 1809. The Fren storming of the Danubian p of Regensburg (above left) u a prelude to the conquest Vienna (top right). In M Archduke Charles Louis led Austrians to a victory over N poleon at Aspern (left). In Ju Charles Louis was defeated Wagram. Above, citizens Vienna aiding the wound after Wagram.

Above, triumphant Napoleonic troops in front of the Schönbrunn, the royal palace in Vienna. Left, the room in the Schönbrunn where Napoleon slept.

had not been forced to prove itself in action for many years. On October 14, 1806, Napoleon happened on a subsidiary force of Prussians near Jena (in present-day East Germany) and gave battle. Believing that he had met and destroyed the Prussian army, the emperor was chagrined to discover that the major battle had been going on simultaneously twelve miles away, where the French general Louis Nicolas Davout had engaged the main body of the Prussians and won despite overwhelming odds. Only twenty-seven days after King Frederick William III of Prussia declared war, the first French troops marched into Berlin.

Prussia was finished, although its king stubbornly refused to admit defeat and sign a treaty. Russia, however, was still very much in the fight, so the Napoleonic army pushed on to Warsaw, where it established winter quarters. From the time of his arrival in Warsaw, Napoleon was surrounded by a party of Polish patriots who hoped that he would rescind the partitions of 1772, 1793, and 1795 and restore their nation's independence. The most fervent entreaties

came from Countess Marie Walewska, a lovely eighteen-year-old who was married to a Polish nobleman in his seventies. Urged on all sides to sacrifice her honor and become Napoleon's mistress for the sake of Poland, the countess won Napoleon's heart but could do little to change his mind. The veteran Polish revolutionary Thaddeus Kosciusko, meanwhile, watched the proceedings with contempt, well aware that Napoleon would never tolerate a strong and independent Polish state. To prolong the hope and loyalty of his Polish supporters, Napoleon established a small duchy of Warsaw, consisting of parts of the formerly Polish territory annexed by Prussia.

Napoleon's winter idyll in Warsaw contrasted cruelly with the scene at the East Prussian town of Eylau, where in February 1807 a fierce battle raged between the French and the allied Russians and Prussians. Forty-five thousand men from both sides lost their lives while fighting in a blinding snowstorm, but the campaign dragged on until the Russo-Prussian defeat at nearby Friedland in June convinced the czar that peace must be made. A few weeks after Friedland, Alexander and Napoleon met on a raft moored in the Neman River near Tilsit—while King Frederick William, Alexander's erstwhile ally, was left waiting on the river bank.

No one knows exactly what Alexander and Napoleon said during their secret meeting on the raft, but clearly each felt that he had deceived and bested the other. Although Alexander gained a breathing space to pursue his foreign policy aims against Sweden and Turkey, his vision of an equal Franco-Russian partnership was mere illusion from the beginning. Napoleon was effusively condescending in his attitude toward the czar. "If he were a woman," the emperor wrote to Joséphine somewhat later, "I would marry him." A few years hence, when Alexander dug in his heels and refused to act as Napoleon's vassal, the alliance collapsed.

After the war of 1805–1807, Napoleon's claims to be the heir of Charlemagne could no longer be dismissed as an empty boast. France had already annexed sizable amounts of territory: Belgium, the left bank of the Rhine, Geneva, and Italian Piedmont. Now Napoleon ceased adding his conquered lands to France proper and began to build a pan-European empire called the Grand Empire. Napoleon's long-term plans for the states of the Grand Empire are uncertain, but his immediate strategy was to exercise control through trusted intermediaries, including former French generals and old supporters, members

Below, the cradle of Napoleon's son, François Charles Joseph, who was called l'Aiglon (the Eaglet).

eft, Napoleon marrying Marie Louise of ustria in 1810, after his divorce from Em-ress Joséphine. Right, Marie Louise and rançois Charles Joseph, the son born to her nd Napoleon in 1811. Below, the emperor nd his new family. Napoleon's son (below ight), reared as an Austrian archduke after apoleon's exile, died at age twenty-one.

of the native ruling classes who had accepted his supremacy, and members of the Bonaparte family.

Napoleon's brothers and sisters were transformed into instant royalty. The intelligent and easygoing Joseph Bonaparte, whom Napoleon had once mockingly called Mr. Equality, became king of Naples. Holland, formerly the Batavian Republic, was made a kingdom for brother Louis and his wife, Hortense de Beauharnais. Joachim Murat, Napoleon's marshal and the husband of Carolina Bonaparte, was named grand duke of Baden, and Jérôme, Napoleon's youngest brother, having repudiated his marriage to Baltimore belle Elizabeth Patterson, became king of Westphalia. Napoleon decided to keep the Kingdom of Italy for himself, but elevated Eugène de Beauharnais, his stepson, to the post of viceroy. A paragon of loyalty in comparison with Napoleon's blood relatives, Eugène was given reason to hope that he would eventually inherit the Italian crown.

The emperor had taken good care of his relatives, but he had absolutely no intention of allowing them

Above, the battle of Borodino, fought in September 1812. Top, A Mounted Officer of the Imperial Guard by Jean Louis André Théodore Géricault. The guard, the elite corps of the Grande Armée, was a special source of pride to Napoleon. During the disastrous winter retreat from Moscow, the emperor made sure that not only the guard but also its horses had sufficient provisions.

govern their new kingdoms as they pleased. He was amant that the Code Napoléon and French institions be introduced throughout the Grand Emre—and since he believed that "there is very little fference between one people and another," he uld accept no excuse for failure.

The personal conduct of the Bonaparte relatives sgusted Napoleon. The marital disputes of Louis d Hortense were an open scandal, and in Westalia Jérôme consoled himself for the loss of Miss tterson by filling his court with fortune-hunting tresses. But what most infuriated Napoleon was his lings' occasional desire to behave as if they actually presented the interests of the peoples they had been med to rule. When Jérôme, who was making a nscientious effort to follow Napoleon's directives, red to complain about the level of taxation, the peror responded impatiently: "I think it is ridicuus for you to tell me that the people of Westphalia not agree. If the people refuse to do what is for eir welfare they are guilty of anarchy."

Nevertheless, it proved impossible to implement Napoleon's complete program everywhere. In the Papal States, occupied in 1807, the secularization of the clergy created hopeless turmoil by destroying the livelihood of the middle class, which had made its living in great part by provisioning churchmen. Some strongly Catholic regions of the Grand Empire objected to the legalization of divorce, while the Dutch quietly but resolutely objected to French domination of their economy.

Despite the many obstacles, the Napoleonic reforms did effect sweeping changes throughout the Grand Empire. Jews and other religious minorities were granted civil rights, and divorce and civil marriage became legal almost everywhere. Tax systems were reformed, and feudal dues, tithes, and internal customs duties were abolished. Courts, secular schools, and postal systems were substantially modernized within a few years. Perhaps most important, careers in the government and army were made accessible to members of the middle class.

Above, the burning of Smolensk in August 1812. Left, the burning of Moscow the following month. News of Moscow's fall only strengthened the czar's resolve to fight. "After this wound," he stated, "all others are trifling."

Internal reforms, important as they were, took second place to Napoleon's goal of imposing a unified foreign policy designed to destroy Britain through economic pressure. Britain and France had used blockades against each other ever since the first phase of the Napoleonic Wars, but the British navy had never abided by the rules generally accepted in Europe. For example, British ships would seize neutral vessels carrying the goods of a belligerent country or would arbitrarily declare certain ports blockaded and then seize ships that had called at these ports while on the open seas. Napoleon's Berlin and Milan decrees of 1806 and 1807 established the new French position regarding the blockade. Any country trading with Britain would be considered the enemy of France and its satellites. The entire Grand Empire and its allies were to participate in the Continental System by refusing to buy goods from Britain.

The goal of the Continental System was not to starve Britain but to deprive it of the opportunity to sell manufactured goods abroad. In theory this would

Top, czarist commanders during the campaign of 18.. At the outset, Prince Pëtr Bagration (left) and Prince N khail Barclay de Tolly (right) had little choice but adopt a policy of retreat. This plan was so unpopul. however, that the aged veteran Prince Mikhail Kutuz (center) was brought out of retirement on the und standing that he would engage the French in battle. K tuzov was defeated at Borodino (above), where Prin Bagration became one of an estimated forty-five thousa. Russian casualties. Above right, French prisoners bei taken to Novgorod.

upset the balance of payments and ruin the Briti economy, producing widespread unemployment, civ unrest, and eventually revolution. In practice, son of Napoleon's most important vassals were relucta to incur enmity by enforcing a policy that would lea to economic hardship. Louis Bonaparte, in particula allowed so many exceptions to the blockade that N. poleon charged him with making Holland a Britis port. Louis was removed from his post in 1810, an Holland and northwestern Germany were annexe

irectly to France. But even in France itself certain xemptions from the boycott were permitted. Mean-hile, smuggling became widespread and Britain earched out new markets in its overseas colonies, outh America, and elsewhere. The British economic ollapse that Napoleon had confidently foreseen ailed to materialize.

In the year after Tilsit, however, it still seemed that othing was beyond Napoleon's reach, including the umbling of Britain. Yet when Napoleon set out to omplete his grand design by subduing the relatively nsignificant kingdom of Portugal, his plans began to nravel.

To close the Portuguese ports, which had become a ajor entry point for British goods, it was necessary o have the cooperation of Spain. At first glance, pain seemed to present few problems. Its king, harles IV, was a powerless figure, totally dominated y Manuel de Godoy, his wife's lover, who had been ro-French since 1796. But in 1807 the heir apparent, rince Ferdinand of Asturias, had become a serious

threat to Godoy's pre-eminence. Napoleon used the power struggle as an excuse to move troops into Spain, leading both factions to believe that he was on their side. In reality, Napoleon had decided on a different solution. In April 1808 he lured Godoy and the royal family to the town of Bayonne in southwestern France, where Charles, Ferdinand, and Godoy were made prisoners. Joseph Bonaparte was then named king of Spain.

The entry of French troops into Madrid sparked the revolt of *dos de Mayo*—May 2, 1808. Within three weeks a violent wave of antiforeign feeling swept over Spain. Insurgent warfare was bitter until the summer, when an English expeditionary corps under General Arthur Wellesley—later the duke of Wellington—arrived to aid the Spanish cause. Napoleon, hastening to Spain to assume command of the French campaign, was able to retake Madrid. But guerrilla fighters, taking advantage of the mountainous terrain, continued to harass the French occupation troops. The British battalions also maintained pres-

"The Dandy King"

The son of a Gascon innkeeper, Joachim Murat came to Napoleon's attention in 1795 and soon became one of his most reliable commanders, undertaking such unsavory tasks as the execution of the duke of Enghien in 1804. Vain and not very intelligent, Murat married Napoleon's sister Carolina, who was second to none at the art of backstairs intrigue. When Joseph Bonaparte became king of Spain, Murat took his brother-in-law's place in Naples.

Unlike the hard-working Joseph, Murat and his queen relied on dazzling pageantry to win the hearts of the Neapolitans.

Deeply offended that Napoleon continued to treat him as an underling, Murat was drawn closer to the Italian nationalists at his court and after 1812 began considering negotiation with the anti-French allies. Upon Napoleon's escape from Elba in early 1815, the vacillating Murat joined Napoleon's cause once again, proclaimed the independence of Italy, and tried to raise a national army to fight Austria. But few Italians cared to risk their lives for such a leader, and Murat's career ended in a quixotic attempt to invade Italy with a few hundred Corsican followers. Taken prisoner, he was shot in October 1815.

Right, Joachim Murat. No one could match Murat in the bravery he displayed on the battlefield or in the figure he cut on the parade ground. Representing Napoleon in the Cisalpine Republic in 1801 (left), he was widely admired. But when he attempted to mount his own invasion of the Anglo-Bourbon island of Capri (below), he failed ignominiously.

Top, an artist's conception of the palace Murat hoped to build in Naples. Immediately above, a room in Murat's palace at Caserta, near Naples. Above left, a clock commemorating Murat's marriage.

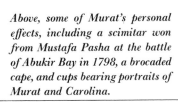

Above, some of Murat's personal effects, including a scimitar won from Mustafa Pasha at the battle of Abukir Bay in 1798, a brocaded cape, and cups bearing portraits of Murat and Carolina.

Right, the edict sentencing Murat to death, issued in 1815 in the name of the restored Bourbon king Ferdinand IV of Naples.

The battle of Leipzig (above), known as t[he]
Battle of the Nations, lasted for three days [in]
October 1813 and paved the way for the [Al-]
lied invasion of France. Left, Austrian troo[ps]
billeted on a French farm in 1814.

Facing page, above, Louis XVIII landing [at]
the French port of Calais in 1814 to resto[re]
the Bourbon monarchy after Napoleon's fa[ll.]
Facing page, below, Czar Alexander accep[t-]
ing the surrender of Paris in 1814. Followi[ng]
pages, Napoleon bidding a tearful farewell [to]
his Imperial Guard before leaving Fontai[ne-]
bleau Palace for Elba, his place of exile.

re on the French, retreating to British navy ships on e coast only to land again a few days later where ey were least expected. The conflict in Spain agged on for years, exacting a terrible price in lives d property and reminding Napoleon's old enemies the east that the fabled Napoleonic army was vul- rable after all.

The Spanish insurrection gave encouragement to e rising tide of German nationalism, and Austria gan to consider reopening the war. Czar Alexander, eanwhile, was increasingly displeased with his wards from the Tilsit agreement. In the autumn of 08, Napoleon met with Alexander at the German ty of Erfurt, doing his best to flatter and cajole the ar. Talleyrand, however, already working quietly hind the scenes for Napoleon's fall, seems to have anted in Alexander's mind the idea that Russia

would gain nothing by supporting France in a war against Austria.

The next spring, emboldened by anti-French in- surrections in the Tyrolean region and northern Ger- many, Austria declared war on France. Napoleon was forced to turn his attention from Spain and take charge of the Army of the Rhine. Under his leader- ship, the Austrians were driven back beyond the Danube and soundly defeated at the battle of Wa- gram in July.

The consequences of Austria's defeat could hardly have been more surprising. The Austrian chancellor, Prince Metternich, seeking to salvage something from the debacle, proposed a marriage between Napoleon and the Hapsburg princess Marie Louise, daughter of the emperor Francis I of Austria and a niece of the ill-fated Queen Marie Antoinette of France. Metter-

Left, a museum on Elba dedicated to Napoleon's memory. Right, a caricature dating from the time of Napoleon's exile. "What a Fall!" exclaims the emperor as his young son weeps inconsolably.

nich's suggestion was irresistible to Napoleon, who desperately wanted a legitimate heir and was certain that Joséphine, then forty-six years old, would never give him a child. A divorce from Josephine was duly arranged, and on April 2, 1810, Napoleon celebrated his marriage to Marie Louise. From now on the emperor was able to refer jokingly to "his uncle" Louis XVI.

Within a year, Marie Louise bore Napoleon a son who was given the title formerly bestowed on the heir apparent to the Holy Roman emperor—"king of Rome." The emperor hoped that his son's Hapsburg ancestry would give his dynasty legitimacy, but the

marriage to Marie Louise only exacerbated Napoleon's problems. Parisian society buzzed with rumo that Louis XVI's memory was to be revived and th the old revolutionaries responsible for his dea would be sent into exile. Napoleon's relatives bristl at the prospect of "their" lands becoming an inher tance for Marie Louise's children. And Czar Ale ander, although he had refused to let his sister mar Napoleon, was not at all pleased that an alternati had been found so easily.

Over the next two years relations between Fran and Russia deteriorated steadily. Russia's particip tion in the Continental System became no more tha

low left, Napoleon's escape from Elba in late February 1815. Below, Napoleon land-g in France. "If there is one among you who uld like to kill his emperor, he may do so," announced. "Here I am!" At this, the sol-rs who had been sent to capture Napoleon l at his feet. Right, Louis XVIII abandon-g the Tuileries palace shortly before Napo-n's arrival in Paris.

minal, and in 1812 Alexander began demanding at Napoleon remove his troops from Prussia and op meddling in Polish affairs. Napoleon, having lit-e respect for Alexander and overweening confidence his own invincibility, decided to settle the problem y invading Russia. Although a sizable force was still gaged in Spain, Napoleon assembled an imperial rande Armée of more than 650,000 men. Only out 200,000 of these were Frenchmen, and the rande Armée of 1812 was aptly described as an my of "twenty nations and twelve languages."

As usual, Napoleon was counting on a short war. ut the Russians kept retreating, drawing their ad-

versary deeper into the deserted interior. The supply corps, which could not even find fodder for the horses that drew its wagons, fell behind the pace. Desertion was rampant, especially among the foreign troops, and the army's main force was soon reduced to about 180,000 soldiers out of an original 450,000. Napoleon's more prudent generals urged a retreat. But Moscow was only two hundred miles away, and Napoleon assumed that the Russians would never surrender Moscow without a fight.

Napoleon was correct. At the last moment, seventy-four-year-old General Mikhail Kutuzov was given command of the Russian army on the understanding that he would engage the Grande Armée in battle. The protracted and bloody confrontation at Borodino on the Moskva River that took place on September 7 was technically a French victory but did nothing to change the pattern of the campaign. A week later, the Napoleonic army caught its first glimpse of the cupolas of the Kremlin, shimmering like a mirage in the distance. When he entered Moscow, Napoleon was shocked to find a deserted city. The night after the French occupation began, Moscow's old wooden buildings were swept by fire, perhaps set by the departing Russian governor. Czar Alexander, safe in St. Petersburg, refused to even consider making peace, so the French had to retreat.

Most of the soldiers who departed from Moscow in October were laden down with booty. (One sergeant recalled having set out with a lady's riding cloak, a jeweled spittoon, a Chinese vase, jewels, and sundry religious treasures.) But before long the troops were eagerly exchanging gold and silver icons for handfuls of grain as they made their way westward across the cold, snowbound expanses during one of the severest winters in memory.

Shaken but not ready to admit defeat, Napoleon stayed with the remnant of the Grande Armée as far as Vilna (in what is now the Lithuanian S.S.R.) and then sped back to Paris, where, after foiling an attempted coup, he began raising another army. Czar Alexander, happy to find himself cast in the heroic role he had always craved, was bent on pursuing Napoleon all the way to Paris. Prussia, Sweden, and eventually Austria joined in what became known as the War of Liberation. By October 1813, Napoleon's attempt to defend his Germany ended in a crushing defeat at the battle of Leipzig, and the Grande Armée was forced back across the Rhine. About the same time, the momentum of the war in Iberia shifted, and the Anglo-Spanish army was moving inexorably closer to the south of France. In spite of these setbacks, Napoleon rejected the offers of the anti-French

Near right, three scenes from the battle of Waterloo, fought in central Belgium on June 18, 1815: top, the siege of the farmhouse at La Haye-Sainte, where the French advance bogged down; center, the Prussians arriving to support the British; and below, the last stand of the French infantry. Waterloo was a triumph for Britain's duke of Wellington (facing page, above left), who had spent years fighting the French on the Iberian Peninsula, and for the Prussian field marshal Gebhard Leberecht von Blücher (facing page, above right), who arrived with his army in time to turn the tide of battle. Below, far right, a plan of the Waterloo battlefield.

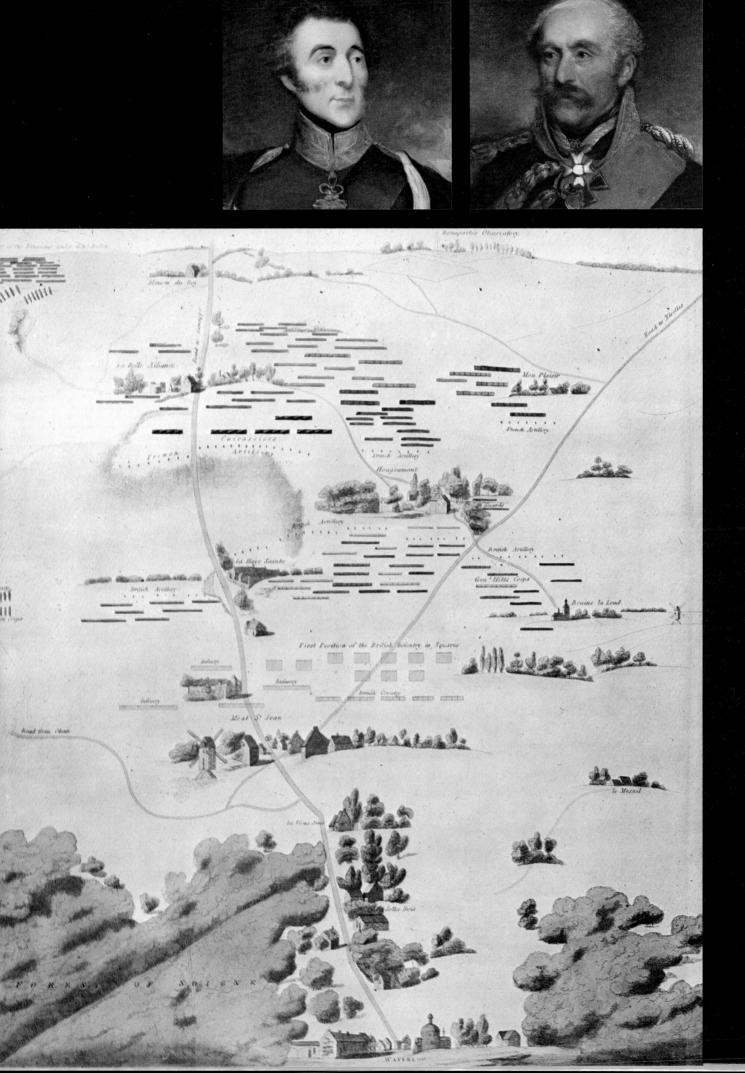

allies that would have left him ruler of France and tried to assemble another army.

As long as Napoleon remained successful and while the burden of manning and outfitting his armies fell substantially on parts of the Napoleonic Empire other than France itself, Frenchmen had been willing to support Napoleon's dreams of glory. But in early 1814, having endured two years of economic depression and belatedly learning the true story of the disastrous Russian campaign, the people simply lost spirit. Army call ups and tax collections ground to a halt, and crowds watched passively as columns of foreign troops marched into France. On April 11, 1814, Napoleon's marshals flatly refused to join him in an attempt to defend Paris, and the emperor abdicated. He was exiled by the Allies to the Mediterranean island of Elba.

When the Allies entered Paris, that wily survivor Talleyrand was on hand to remind the victors that Napoleon was their enemy but that the French people were not. The plan Talleyrand advanced for post-Napoleonic France, however, bore little relation to what the French people wanted. Louis XVIII, a brother of the last king, was placed on the throne and agreed to rule as a constitutional monarch. But the return of the Bourbon pretender and his ultramonarchist followers, who after twenty years of plotting abroad had "learned nothing and forgotten nothing," aroused widespread misgivings. Louis XVIII's most brazen offense to public opinion was his replacement of France's tricolor with the white flag of the Bourbons. France seethed with plots, and on February 15, Napoleon escaped from his island exile.

He arrived on the mainland with only one thousand followers and four small cannons, but local garrisons, retired army men, and republican peasants and workers quickly flocked to his banner. Paris newspapers chronicled the approach of this makeshift army in a series of revealing headlines—"The Ogre Has Landed" and "The Usurper Is on the March," followed by "Bonaparte Advances," and finally, "His Majesty the Emperor Re-enters Paris." By this time,

Right, a detail of the Great Shield of Wellington, created to commemorate the victory of Waterloo. Wellington, shown on horseback at center, is being crowned with a laurel wreath.

the ineffectual Louis XVIII had quietly slipped across the border into Belgium.

Incredibly, the tricolor was flying over Paris once again. The French people were prepared to forgive Napoleon, but they were not willing to return to authoritarian rule. "That blackguard [Louis XVIII] has ruined France for me," Napoleon complained, caught between the demands of the old nobles and the upper middle class who had supported the Bourbon restoration and the expectations of the republicans who had helped him return to power.

Napoleon's belief that the Allied powers would accept his resurrection as a *fait accompli* proved to be ill founded. Two of the armies that had occupied France in 1814 were still in Belgium, and Napoleon decided to gamble everything on destroying them. To bolster the French army he resorted to conscription, and even his marshals and closest supporters watched with some apprehension as the old soldier who had returned from Elba began acting more and more like the arrogant emperor of the past.

Napoleon's Belgian campaign was only three days old when he lost his army to the duke of Wellington's forces at the town of Waterloo. Even then he refused to admit defeat and rushed back to Paris, where he talked about assembling another army until the exasperated Fouché—once again minister of police—threatened to arrest him if he did not flee. After trying unsuccessfully to find a ship that would take him to the United States, he surrendered to the British.

This time the British took no chances. General Bonaparte (he was no longer to be addressed as Napoleon) was shipped off to the island of St. Helena in the South Atlantic, where he lived under house arrest. Napoleon's active career was over, but his genius for propaganda remained in top form. Although the conditions of his exile were fairly comfortable, he and his remaining supporters managed to spread the impression that the former French emperor was suffering grievously at the hands of the heartless British.

Even the pope, who had himself suffered imprisonment at the hands of the Napoleonic army, was roused to plead on his old tormentor's behalf.

In truth, Napoleon's worst privations were imposed by his own unbending pride. He gave up the privilege of riding horseback around the island because he could not bear the humiliation of being followed by a British guard, and he refused to admit the British governor to his presence. Housebound and isolated, he spent much of his time brooding over the desertion of his empress, Marie Louise, who had wasted little time in taking as her lover the Austrian officer appointed to watch over her. Napoleon's son, the former king of Rome, was now in the hands of his enemies and was being raised as an Austrian archduke. Bitter as it was, the separation from his family made it easier for Napoleon to forget that he had ever craved the acceptance of the established ruling families of Europe.

Napoleon's *Memoirs* and the reminiscences of those who visited him at St. Helena created a legendary Napoleon who was a martyr of the Revolution,

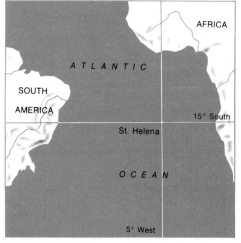

Above, Longwood House on the island of St. Helena in the South Atlantic, where Napoleon lived until his death in 1821. Facing page, below (left to right): a map showing the location of St. Helena, a view of Napoleon's dining room, and Napoleon's bedroom. Although Napoleon complained frequently about the distressful conditions of his imprisonment, he lived in relative comfort.

Right, Napoleon in exile. A British officer's wife who met Napoleon during this period was surprised to find, instead of the ogre she had expected, a plump, querulous little man who seemed much older than his years. Napoleon was only fifty-one when he died of stomach cancer, a condition aggravated by the harsh remedies his doctor had prescribed to cure his chronic ulcers.

peace-loving ruler waging war only in response to aggression. Absent from these writings was the image of a man who had imposed a tyrannical regime on France, played with the hopes of patriots in Italy, Germany, and Poland, and sacrificed many thousands (an estimated seventy thousand yearly from France alone) to the pursuit of glory.

After Napoleon's abdication in 1814, his empire was dismantled and the Congress of Vienna (1814–1815) redrew the map of Europe to restore the balance of power. Ironically, the conservatism of the congress participants did much to enhance the legend of Napoleon Bonaparte, son of the Revolution. In France, which was weighed down but hardly chastened by the burdens of defeat and reparations, Napoleon was widely remembered as the great man who had pursued the war initiated by the Revolution's enemies and led France to a pinnacle of military supremacy. Between 1848 and 1852 these memories gained enough momentum to propel Louis Bonaparte's son to the throne as Napoleon III and inspire the ill-fated policies of the Second Empire, which culminated in the humiliating defeat of France during the Franco-Prussian War of 1870–1871.

On the European continent as a whole, the legacy of Napoleonic reforms and the Code Napoléon remained as symbols of the death of feudalism and the triumph of the property-owning middle class. Because of Napoleon, the number of states in Germany had been drastically reduced; Poland had reappeared as a constitutional monarchy, though under Russian hegemony; and the Low Countries had acquired constitutions based on French models. In the Western Hemisphere, where Napoleon had attempted unsuccessfully to reconquer Hispaniola and restore the slave trade, he was recalled primarily as the man who had sold the Louisiana Territory to the United States and given encouragement to Latin American independence movements.

The prisoner of St. Helena died in 1821, at the age of fifty-one. He left behind a legend tenacious but contradictory. It is quite possible to contend that the developments associated with Napoleon—the transformation of France into a one-man dictatorship, the endless wars, the advance of the middle class—would have occurred even if Napoleon had never risen to power. However logical such arguments may be, they have done little to dim the allure of Napoleon the self-made genius, the supreme individualist who shaped history rather than allowing history to shape him.

Photography Credits

Jörg P. Anders: p. 21 bottom left, p. 67 top, p. 72 top left and center left / *Arborio-Mella:* p. 49 left, pp. 52–53 / *Archiv für Kunst und Geschichte:* p. 14, p. 16 top, p. 23 top, p. 24 bottom left, pp. 24–25 center, p. 26 top, p. 36 center, p. 41 bottom right, p. 44 bottom, p. 45 bottom, p. 49 top, p. 56 bottom left, p. 61, p. 66, p. 71 top left, p. 81 center, pp. 84–85 top center, p. 106 top left / *Bavaria:* p. 21 top / *Bavaria-Fiore:* p. 35 center / *Bavaria-W. Meier:* p. 35 bottom / *Bavaria-Puck-Kornetzki:* p. 18 top / *Bildarchiv Preussischer Kulturbesitz:* p. 12 top, p. 13 top, p. 15 top, p. 16 bottom, p. 17, p. 22, p. 23 bottom, p. 28 left, p. 29 top left and bottom left, p. 30 top and center, p. 31, pp. 36–37 center, p. 39 top left, p. 40, p. 41 top and bottom left, p. 47, p. 55 right, pp. 64–65, p. 69, p. 70, p. 71 bottom, pp. 74–75, p. 76 top left, p. 78 top left, p. 79 top, p. 81 top and bottom, p. 82 top, p. 83 top left, p. 84 bottom left and right, p. 87 / *Bildarchiv Preussischer Kulturbesitz-J. Bartsch:* p. 46, p. 72 bottom left, p. 77 / *Bildarchiv Preussicher Kulturbesitz-Frewel:* p. 19 right, pp. 30–31 center / *Bildarchiv Preussischer Kulturbesitz-R. Walz:* p. 15 center / *Bavaria-Kanus:* p. 11 bottom left / *Allan Cash:* p. 93 bottom left and right / *Costa:* p. 20, p. 50, p. 51, p. 76 top right, p. 82 bottom, p. 83 center and bottom, p. 85 top right and bottom right, p. 91, p. 101 bottom right, p. 111 top and bottom left, pp. 116–117 top, p. 117 bottom left, p. 124 top left and bottom, p. 125 bottom right, p. 129 top, p. 131 top, p. 132 left and bottom right, p. 133 right and bottom left, pp. 142–143 bottom, p. 144 top and bottom left, p. 153, p. 154 top, p. 160 top right, p. 162 bottom, p. 167 / *Dulevant:* p. 97 center, p. 99 bottom left, p. 141 top left, p. 161 bottom, p. 166 top / *Foto 2000:* p. 106 top right, p. 116 bottom, p. 117 right center / *Giraudon:* pp. 142–143 top center, p. 163 bottom / *Giraudon-Lauros:* p. 95 bottom center, p. 118 right, pp. 132–133 top center, p. 150 bottom right / *Hassmann:* p. 9, p. 28 right, p. 29 top right and bottom right, p. 30 bottom, pp. 32–33, p. 34, p. 38, pp 44–45 top, p. 56 top and bottom right, p. 57, p. 145 bottom, p. 146 bottom, p. 156 bottom / *Gloria Lunel:* p. 18 center and bottom, p. 19 bottom left, p.21 bottom right, p. 25 bottom right, p. 68, p. 76 bottom / *Magnum-Lessing:* p. 13 bottom, p. 39 top right and bottom right, p. 67 bottom, p. 89, p. 104 bottom, pp. 120–121, p. 126, p. 129 bottom right, p. 137 bottom, p. 138 left and bottom right, p. 139 top and bottom right, p. 145 top, first from left, p. 147, p. 162 top and center / *Mairani:* p. 60, p. 142 top left, p. 160 top left, p. 166 bottom left and right / *Meyer:* p. 62 top right, p. 106 bottom left / *Novosti:* p. 152 / *R. Pedicini:* p. 155 / *Pucciarelli:* p. 94 top, p. 95 right, p. 99 right center, p. 101 bottom left, p. 105 right, third row from top, p. 107, p. 112 top left and right, p. 112 bottom, p. 113, p. 122 top right, p. 149 top left / *Reinhold:* p. 62 bottom left and right, p. 63 top and bottom / *Remmer:* p. 71 top right, p. 78 top right and bottom, p. 79 bottom / *Ricatto:* p. 104 top / *Ricciarini:* p. 90 top, p. 138 top right / *Ricciarini-Arch. B:* p. 94 bottom, p. 97 top center / *Ricciarini-Simion:* p. 96, p. 97 top left, p. 98 left, p. 100 top, p. 103, p. 119, p. 143 right center, p. 145 top, second from left / *Ricciarini-Tomsich:* p. 104, p. 105 center and left, second from top, p. 143 top right / *Lores Riva:* p. 80, p. 84 top left, p. 151, p. 157 bottom / *Rizzoli:* p. 83 top right, p. 90 bottom left and right, p. 95 top left, p. 97 top right and bottom, p. 98 bottom right, p. 99 top left, and right, and bottom right, p. 100 bottom, p. 106 center right and bottom right, p. 108 bottom, p. 109, p. 111 bottom right, p. 112 center, pp. 114–115, p. [...] bottom right, p. 118 left, p. 122 bottom, p. 1[...] pp. 124–125 top center, p. 125 top right, p. [...] center, p. 128, p. 129 bottom left, p. 140 botto[...] right, p. 141 bottom, p. 143 bottom right, p. [...] top, last on right, p. 148, p. 149 bottom right, [...] 157 top, pp. 158–159, p. 163 top right, pp. 16[...] 165 / *Scala:* p. 111 bottom center / *SEF:* p. [...] top / *Stern-Thomann:* p. 10, p. 11 top right, [...] 10–11 top center, p. 12 bottom, p. 15 bottom, [...] 24 top and bottom right, p. 27 top and center, [...] 26–27 bottom, p. 35 top, p. 36 top and bottom, [...] 37 top right and bottom right, pp. 42–43, p. 48, [...] 54, p. 55 left, pp. 72–73 top center / *Titus:* [...] top left and center, p. 73 bottom, p. 95 top cent[...] p. 102, p. 108 top, p. 122 top left, p. 127 top a[...] bottom, p. 130, p. 131 center and bottom, p. [...] top and bottom, p. 137 top, p. 138 bottom left, [...] 139 bottom left, p. 140 left and top right, p. 1[...] top right, p. 144 bottom right, p. 145 top, thi[...] from left, p. 146 top left, top right, and center, [...] 149 top right and bottom left, p. 150 left and t[...] right, p. 154 bottom, pp. 154 155 center, p. 1[...] top, p. 163 top left / *Titus-Beaujard:* p. 92, p. [...] top / *Versailles, Musée de la Ville:* p. 160 bottom[...] *Zefa-Hille:* p. 63 center / *Zefa-Kramarz:* p. 11 b[...] tom right / *Zefa-Paul:* p. 25 top right